CHINA'S FIRST EMPEROR PREPARATION FOR THE AFTERLIFE

The Entombed Terra-cotta Warriors and Other Underground Chambers, Containing Replicas of Earthly Life

Written in Chinese by Zhang Tao
English translated by Liu Daoxuan
and Zhang Tao
English proof read by Robert Dorning(Australia)

(陕)新登字 012 号
责任编辑:臧　云
责任监制:刘青海

CHINA'S FIRST EMPEROR

PREPARATION

FOR THE AFTERLIFE

The Entombed Terra-cotta
Warriors and Other
Underground Chambers,
Containing Replicas of
Earthly Life

Author of the Chinese Version: Zhang Tao
Translators: Liu Daoxuan and Zhang Tao
Proof reader: Robert Dorning (Australia)
Photographers: Xia Juxian and Guo Yan

陕西旅游出版社出版发行
(西安长安路 32 号　邮政编码 710061)
新华书店经销　西安创意设计印务有限责任公司印刷
787×1092mm　32 开本　5.75 印张　16 插页　140 千字
2002 年 4 月第 1 版　2002 年 4 月第 1 次印刷
印数:1—2,000
ISBN 7—5418—1846—1/J·440
定价:15.00

读者如发现印、装质量问题,请与印厂联系调换
厂址:西安市太白南路规划路 2 号　邮编:710068　电话:8231355

The mausoleum of Qin Shihuang,the Qin First Emperor

The Exhibition Hall of Cultural Relics from the Qin Mausoleum

Semi-naked terra-cotta figures depicting theatrical performe

A stone helmet excavated recently
from the Qin Mausoleum garden

Bronze tripod excavate
from the Qin Mausoleu

xcavated recently from the qin mausoleum garden

ecently
garden

Stone armour excavated recently from
the Qin Mausoleum garden

No.1 bronze chariot

No.2 bronze chariot

A terra-cotta charioteer

A terra-cotta warrior holding the reins of a horse

A kneeling painted terra-cotta atcher excavated recently from Vault Ⅱ

A green-faced head of a warrior excavated recently from Vault Ⅱ

A terra-cotta senior army officer

A terra-cotta archer in the pose of shooting a bow and arrow

A terra-cotta senior army officer

A terra- cotta warrior
with armour

Outside view of Vault II

Panoramic view of Vault II

Outside view of Vault III

Panoramic view of Vault III

Qutside view of Vault Ⅰ

Panoramic view of Vault Ⅰ

Panoramic view of Vault Ⅰ

Panoramic view of Vault I

ABOUT THE AUTHOR

ZHANG TAO, born in Xi'an, China in 1965, has worked at the Museum of Terra – cotta Warriors and Horses of Emperor Qin Shihuang since he graduated from the Department of History of a university in 1988.

At the Museum he has been involved in the preparation of exhibitions and research into the history of the State of Qin, the First Emperor's Mausoleum and the Qin terra – cotta statues.

He has published more than 20 essays and a number of books on the history, the Mausoleum and the terra – cotta statues of the Qin Dynasty. The books are "Qin Shihuang's Terra – cotta Warriors and Horses", "Three Discoveries around the Qin Mausoleum", "Marvelous Underground Troops – Terra – cotta Warriors and Horses of the Qin First Emperor", "Study of the Terra – cotta Figures of Qin" and "Study of the Qin Mausoleum".

Amongst these works the "Qin Shihuang's Terra – cotta Warriors and Horses" was listed at the top of the best books published in a month by "China Times". Also Professor Zhang Guangzhi at Harvard University, USA commended it for both its pictures and text with its rich content but simple explanations and deep knowledge.

　　Zhang Tao accompanied an Exhibition of the Qin Terra－cotta Figures to the Birmingham Museum of Art in Alabama, USA during the Olympic year of 1996. He was interviewed by several media outlets in America. He visited Australia for lecture with Mr. Wu, his Director in 2000.

PREFACE

By Wu Yongqi,
Director, Museum of the Terra – cotta Warriors
and Horses of Emperor Qin Shihuang

Located 30 kilometres east of Xi'an, China, the Qin Mausoleum is the largest Tomb Garden of the Emperors in the history of Ancient China. Qin Shihuang (259 to 210 B. C.) was the First Emperor of the Qin Dynasty, who for the first time in Chinese history united the country under a centrally – ruled state. The Qin Dynasty lasted only 15 years from 221 to 206 B. C., but it laid the political foundation for the next 2000 years of feudal society, and greatly influenced the development of the history of Ancient China.

Emperors began to build their mausoleums as soon as they ascended the throne in ancient times. It took about 38 years to construct the Qin Mausoleum and around 800,000 people took part in its construction. The Qin Mausoleum is famous for its unique shape, huge size and special and rich burial objects.

The discovery of the Terra – cotta Army in the Qin Mausoleum stirred the world in 1970s. The Terra – cotta Army is buried in three vaults, covering an area of over 20,000 square metres. More than 8000 terra – cotta warriors and horses, over one hundred wooden chariots and about 20,000 bronze weapons will be unearthed from these vaults. The excavation and archaeological research of the Qin Mausoleum have been carried out according to a plan and by now about 600 attendant vaults have been excavated and 50,000 important relics unearthed. We are sure that additional new discoveries will be made as the excavation continues. The Qin Mausoleum and its Terra – cotta Army have been placed by the UN among the world's cultural legacies and the excavation and protection of the Terra – cotta Army was awarded International Aunas of Greece. The Terra – cotta Army has been named the Eighth Wonder of the World.

The book written in Chinese by Mr. Zhang Tao, a museologist at our museum, systematically introduces the Qin Mausoleum, the Terra – cotta Army, the bronze chariots and recent discoveries such as the stone armour and helmet, the Qin tripod (a bronze three legged vessel), semi naked terra – cotta figures, kneeling colour – painted archers and the history of the Qin Dynasty concerning the Qin First Emperor as well.

The book contains rich content and photographs. It was translated into English by Mr. Liu Daoxuan, an interpreter and translator in the Foreign Affairs Office of the Xianyang Municipal People's Government and Zhang Tao, the author himself. It was proof read by Mr. Robert Dorning, an Australian friend. The book is technical reading material about the Qin Dynasty. I hope you enjoy reading it.

CONTENTS

PROLOGUE
By Robert Dorning, Proof - reader

This new book is written by Zhang Tao, a museologist at the museum set up on the excavation site of the Entombed Terra - cotta Warriors. The book contains completely new material about archaeological discoveries for the non - specialist English - speaking reader. Even for a China specialist it could contain information about, and photographs of, things previously poorly explained, or which have been discovered only in recent years. It contains material previously unavailable outside of China.

The burial mound (tumulus) of Emperor Qin Shihuang, China's First Emperor (259 to 210 B. C.), had been a prominent landmark over the centuries and from historical records it was known to be his burial place. However, there wasn't any record of the associated underground structures. The chance discovery only 26 years ago of the vast underground Terra - cotta Army was totally unexpected. The Museum of the Terra - cotta Warriors and Horses of Emperor Qin Shihuang was established to excavate, restore and exhibit the terra - cotta figures.

The Museum has had considerable success, not only in

excavating and restoring the warriors, horses and chariots, but also in delineating the extent and number of other underground chambers containing replicas from the world of the living. So far, around 600 pits have been discovered within the confines of the necropolis which spreads over a large area of over two square kilometres.

There are details of new discoveries published in this book and new information about previously announced underground chambers. The new discoveries include the eleven member acrobatic troupe and the beautiful stone armour and helmets in what may have been an underground armoury. The new information previously unavailable to the non – specialist is a fuller explanation of the large number of underground stables located around the Mausoleum in which many horses were buried alive. There is also greater explanation of the vaults of rare birds and strange animals, but the picture of these is still not totally clear.

As becomes evident from the book, as the products of excavation are worked up, and new discoveries are described, it becomes clearer that the contents of these other "pits" mean they, also, were underground chambers each imitating particular aspects of the world of the living. For the western observer, the meaning of these underground chambers and their occupants is an intriguing question.

The Qin Mausoleum was not built by survivors of Qin Shihuang hoping to benefit by erecting an edifice to a departed, but powerful leader. Apart from at the beginning after his ascent to the throne as a boy, construction of the Mausoleum was overseen by the man who was to be the subject of this burial preparation. With construction proceeding throughout his life and demanding huge resources from the treasury it cannot be viewed as a light undertaking without deep meaning.

It is not totally clear how the afterlife was perceived in ancient China, or what was the precise role of the occupants of the underground chambers.

Certainly, there was a strong belief in the afterlife. There has been the long practice of ancestor worship with sacrifices and offerings of food and drink to the departed. Fulfilling of filial obligations to the spirits of the dead encouraged action in the other world on behalf of the survivor. Alternatively, failure to do so might lead to vengeful retribution. There was also the belief in ghosts where the spirit of the dead failed to pass over into the other world and remained in the present appearing as an apparition.

It seems as if the spirit of the dead entered a netherworld, a shadowy underground world where funerary objects would serve, succour and protect the spirit as when alive. This netherworld was known at different stages as "Yellow Springs", or "Nine Springs".

Inclusion of grave goods used during the deceased's lifetime had been an early practice in Chinese history (as in other cultures). During the Neolithic period (8th to 2nd

Millennium B. C.), objects such as pottery, weapons, tools and ornaments, were interred so they could be employed in the hereafter.

Towards the end of the Neolithic age there is evidence of human sacrifice in burials. During the succeeding Shang Dynasty (16th to 11th Century B. C.) the scale of human and animal sacrifice grew to considerable proportions with over 300 human corpses found in some tombs near the end of this dynasty. Either buried alive, or killed before entombment, officials, guards, concubines, servants and slaves could be forced to accompany the coffin to serve to their lord as they had in life.

During this time, pottery and jade figures of people and animals were also used as tomb goods. In the Western Zhou Dynasty (11th Century to 771 B. C.) and through into the Warring States Period (475 to 221 B. C.), human sacrifice continued, but declined and eventually was largely abandoned.

Funerary figures came to replace the live people and animals entombed in noble burials. There was a strong moral argument for not practising this cruel practice, but it may well also have become accepted that replicas could fulfill the role better than living beings. After all people and animals die and decompose, whereas long lasting statues can be sculptured to the desired shape to depict unmistakably the intended role and attitude. These statues would render the same service beyond the grave as did their models in the living world.

It is reported that Emperor Qin Shihuang had a superstitious nature, a dread of death and pursued a prolonged quest for immortality. Expecting to be emperor in the next world he ordered construction of a necropolis with extensive above ground structures and numerous subterranean chambers housing figures modelled from the life he knew.

The First Emperor's physical remains would lie in his reputedly spectacular burial chamber, but his spirit would be supported beyond the grave, in their intended roles, by the occupants of the various underground chambers spread around the necropolis.

The underground terra – cotta army prepared the western world for the scale of the First Emperor's mortuary complex. However, when the underground army was the only well – described underground ensemble it created a particularly military, or martial, cast to our understanding of the First Emperor's preparation for the afterlife (in line with his military exploits).

Much of the Mausoleum had been looted, or damaged by vandalism, fire, time, erosion or collapse of underground chambers. The book provides an overview of the large mortuary complex (of which the Entombed Warriors are a part) and the number and variety of underground chambers discovered so far. While the impression is still predominantly military it suggests a richer view of the mortuary complex. To the imaginative mind it hints at what has not yet been discovered and what could have been lost forever.

Other vaults that have been discovered indicate that underground chambers were also created containing figures depicting the Emperor's daily (non – military) life. The recently discovered eleven figure acrobatic troupe would provide lively entertainment for the Emperor and guests. The pits of rare birds and strange animals (discovered in 1977 and '78) are interpreted to represent the imperial parks and forests where the Emperor's party could relax and hunt. A pit discovered in 1996 contains bones of numerous birds, animals and fish. Will future discoveries and excavations find scenes of say palace, or house – hold, life showing possibly how extensive was the preparation for the hereafter?

This book provides glimpses into, and suggests ideas about, how the overall mortuary complex may have been perceived by its designers and the man who built it and for whom it was built. It gives the reader an insight into how life after death may have been viewed by the elite in China in that period.

For English – speaking readers the new book is a welcome addition to information on a unique monument which provides so much insight into a civilisation so different to modern culture. The new information presented in this book confirms the predictions that there would be exciting new discoveries in addition to the underground army and gives even greater promise of more treasures to be discovered in the future.

I. THE RISE OF
THE QIN PEOPLE

According to legend Nu Xiu, the ancestorial mother of the Qin people, was a descendant of Zhuan Xu , who was also called Gaoyang. He was the grandson of the Yellow Emperor, one of the Five Great Emperors in Chinese history. Inscriptions on a stone bell excavated from No. 1 Tomb of a Qin Duke in Fengxiang County, Shaanxi Province said, "Gonghuan is an offspring and Gaoyang's soul is in heaven". This showed the Qin people considered themselves as offspring of Gaoyang. Nu Xiu had become pregnant after she had eaten an egg of a swallow, and so the picture of a swallow became a symbol of the Qin tribe. Nu Xiu's son was Da Ye and Da Ye had a son called Da Fei.

THE QIN PEOPLE GREW AND
BUILT A KINGDOM

When Da Fei was head of the Qin tribe, he helped King Shun raise birds and animals. Because of this good work, King Shun gave him the surname of Ying. At the end of Xia Dynasty (about 21st to 16th century B. C.), Fei Chang, the great grandson of Da Fei left Xia Jie and went to Shang (Shang Dynasty: about 16th to 11th century B. C.) and fought with the Shang against the cruel Xia Jie. In the middle of the Western Zhou Dynasty (about 11th century to 771 B. C.) the Qin people lived in Tianshui, now Gansu Province. Fei Zi, an ancestor of the Qin people was good at raising horses and was asked by King Xiao of Zhou to come into Huiwei (now Guizhen Town, Baoji, Shaanxi Province) to raise horses for the imperial court. He did an excellent job and was made a relative of the King who bestowed him a territory "Qin" (east of Qingshui, now Gansu Province) called Qin Ying. Since then people with the surname Ying were call the Qin people and they had their own conferred territory.

At the end of the Western Zhou Dynasty, King You was fatuous and cruel. He adored his concubine Bao Shi and in order to make her smile he once sent his men to set a signal fire on the platform on Mount Lishan. His generals and dukes saw the fire and thinking their capital was under threat hurriedly lead troops there, but found it to be a joke. When a real enemy attacked the capital in 770 B. C., King You had the fire set again, but this time his generals and dukes thought it was a joke. King You was killed at the foot of Mount Lishan and the Western Zhou Dynasty ended. King Ping of Zhou moved his capital to Lueyi (now Lueyang City, Henan Province) and was accompanied by Qin Xianggong who was made a duke and had a large piece of land in the west of Qishan bestowed to him because of his contribution to the Court. After that the Qin people began to establish their own state.

WHERE DID THE NAME "CHINA" COME FROM?

"China" is a simple translation of the Chinese word "Zhongguo" which has never altered although dynasties changed one after another in Chinese history. "China" was recorded in many foreign languages such as Indian, Greek, Latin and Arabic. The ancient civilized countries like India, Greece and Rome and modern developed countries like Britain, France, German and Japan, who had contacts with China, almost all used "China" to mean this country.

Why do foreigners use "China" for "Zhongguo"? There have been discussions among scholars both at home and abroad. There are several explanations but mainly they say:

a) it came from sound of "Qin" (pronounced "chin"),

b) China was where china was first made.

Matinus Maktini (1614 to 1647) was an Italian missionary who came to China for missionary work in the first half of the 17th century. His Chinese name was Wei Kuang Guo and he was one of the western missionaries who first studied and surveyed Chinese geography and drew a map of China. The "New Atlas", compiled by geographer Jone Buluo, was published in Holland in 1665 and "The New Map of China" drawn by Wei Kuang Guo (Maktini) was in it. In the description it was said for the first time that "China" came from the sound of "Qin". "China" or "Chinas" appeared in Indian poems written in the 5th century B. C.

THE QIN STATE DEFEATED OTHER TRIBES AND STATES

The Qin people had the territory bestowed by King Ping of Zhou, but on this land there also lived the Shu and Di tribes. After fighting them for over 10 years, the Qin people gained control and settled. After 3 generations of dukes in over 80 years, a strong Qin state was built with its centre in now Shaanxi Province, the western boundary in now Tianshui, Gansu Province and the eastern boundary in now Hua County, Shaanxi Province.

In 677 B. C Duke Qin De moved the capital of the Qin State from a narrow valley at Pingyang (now Pingyang town, Baoji, Shaanxi Province) to the plain at Rongcheng (now Fengxiang County, Shaanxi Province). Rongcheng served as the capital of the Qin State for 294 years until 383 B. C. and about 20 generations of dukes lived there. During this period the Qin State, with rich land, became stronger and stronger, and Duke Qin Mu was one of 5 powerful dukes in the Spring and Autumn Period (770 to 476 B. C.). Many remains were discovered around Rongcheng and stone drums, bronze

1 - 1   Calligraphy on a stone (rubbing)

construction materials, tile ends, jade, gold were excavated. These discoveries and excavations showed there used to be many magnificent palaces in Rongcheng.

1－2   Roof tile－end with a deer and wild goose design

Duke Qin Xian succeeded to the throne in 384 B. C. and was a great king. He revoked the rule of burying living slaves with their dead masters one year after his succession. To do battle with the Wei State, he moved his capital from Rongcheng to Leyang (now Lintong Xi' an, Shaanxi Province), showing his determination to defeat the Wei. Also he moved to be away from the interference of the old power and begin his reforms. After moving the capital, he issued the "first field as a business" decree, thereby allowing business activities in 378 B. C. , speeding up the end of old productive

1 - 3   Gilt bronze wine vessel in a garlic shape

relationships. He also carried out "a system of five families as a unit" to raise the position of slaves. He set up a county administrative system in 375 B. C. . The Qin's military force became strong and defeated the Wei army at Leyang (now Dali

County, Shaanxi Province) and Shimen (now Yuncheng, Shanxi Province) in 366 B. C.. The victory in battle changed the "easy to be defeated" appearance of the Qin State.

Duke Qin Xiao succeeded the throne after the death of Qin Xian. He planned to follow the course set by his father and make the state stronger. He issued several decrees to attract talented people and Shang Yang came to the Qin State from the Wei State. As Prime Minister from 359 B. C. to 350 B. C. Shang Yang assisted Duke Qin Xiao to carry out a series of reforms, which are called "Shang Yang's Reform" in Chinese history. The reform sped up the change of economic structure, promoted development of society and formed a centralized political system. It created a solid foundation for the powerful Qin State and its unification of the whole country.

Duke Qin Hui came to the throne after Qin Xiao and he defeated the Wei army in Diaoyin (now Mixian County, Shaanxi Province).

After several generations, the State of Qin successively conquered the states of Han, Zhao, Wei, Yan, Chu and Qi, all six strong states, ending the warfare and unifying China by 221 B. C.. A new page had been opened in Chinese history. Although the Qin Dynasty lasted only 15 years, it greatly influenced Chinese feudal society.

II. QIN SHIHUANG, THE FIRST EMPEROR IN CHINESE HISTORY

On a day in January, 259 B.C. a boy was born in Handan (now Handan City, Hebei Province) to the family of Yi Ren. Handan was the capital of the State of Zhao. Named Ying Zheng, the baby was to become the First Emperor of China.

QIN SHIHUANG'S EARLY LIFE AND HOW HE UNIFIED CHINA

The father Yi Ren was a grandson of King Qin Zhao and had 20 brothers. However, he wasn't the eldest son and his mother wasn't the favourite concubine of the Prince. In 279 B.C. King Qin Zhao wished to centralize his forces to attack the State of Chu, but he was afraid that he would be attacked from behind by the State of Zhao. So he met with King Zhao Hui in Mianchi and sent his grandson as a "hostage" to the State of Zhao. After the Qin had defeated the State of Chu, the Zhao and the Qin began to fight.

Yi Ren, still a hostage, was in danger, but a merchant and far-sighted politician, Lu Buwei, assisted him. Lu Buwei knew that King Qin Zhao was old and Crown Prince Xiao Wen

2-1   Statue of the Qin First Emperor

would succeed him. Xiao Wen's favourite concubine Hua Yang
would become Queen, but she didn't have a son and who
would be the Crown Prince? Lu Buwei gave Yi Ren much gold

for him to buy many unique gifts for Hua Yang and for him to make friends with high officials. So that Hua Yang would become fond of him, Yi Ren changed his name into Zi Chu. Subsequently, Zi Chu was entitled the Crown Prince.

While Yi Ren was living in the State of Zhao, he married Zhao Ji with the help of Lu Buwei and they had a son named Ying Zheng (who was Qin Shihuang later). A legend had it that Qin Shihuang was really the son of Lu Buwei because Zhao Ji was pregnant when she married Yi Ren. So there are still arguments about the life story of Qin Shihuang.

Zi Chu (Yi Ren) eventually succeeded to the throne of the Qin Kingdom and was called King Zhuang Xiang. Lu Buwei was appointed Prime Minister. But King Zhuang Xiang died mysteriously after only 3 years. Crown Prince Ying Zheng, aged 13, succeeded him and appointed Lu Buwei Prime Minister and called him "God Father".

"Historical Records" written by Sima Qian in 100 B. C. said Zhao Ji became the mother of the King when she was young. Initially she had secret communications with Lu Buwei and later had a young man, Lao Ai, live with her at the Court with whom she had two sons. Because Ying Zheng was too young to administer the country two factions formed in the Court – one was the Officials Party led by Lu Buwei and the other was associated with the King's mother and led by Lao Ai. The two factions fought each other for control of the Court.

Ying Zheng's brother Cheng Jiao was the first to challenge for the throne. He led an army against the State of Zhao in 239 B. C. , but on the way rebelled and returned to fight against the Court. He was defeated and killed.

In 238 B. C. , at the age of 22, Ying Zheng was coronated. Lao Ai tried to lead an army against the Qin King but the King attacked first and killed Lao Ai by horse dragging. (One of ways how the prisoner was killed in ancient time. − The prisoner was tied by arms and legs with four horses, and were dragged by the horses to four directions.) The Qin King had his two stepbrothers killed and his mother Zhao Ji was placed under house arrest in a palace. Prime Minister Lu Buwei was dismissed and sent to (now) Henan Province. Two years later King Qin wrote to Lu Buwei, "What contribution did you make to the Qin Dynasty? Why were you conferred a large piece of land? Why were you called 'God Father'?" On receiving the letter, Lu Buwei knew he would be assassinated so he committed suicide. So the internal struggle for the throne ended, but Qin Shihuang's life story remained a secret.

After the coronation and victory with the struggle for the throne, King Qin appointed Li Si Prime Minister and made Wang Jian and his son generals. He carried out the strategy of "making friends with distance states and fighting against neighbouring states" and he conquered the six states Han, Zhao, Wei, Chu, Yan and Qi successively from 230 B. C. to

2 - 2   Sculptures suggesting the Qin First Emperor unifying China

221 B. C.. He established the first united centrally - ruled feudal country. After the unification he named himself Qin Shihuang (meaning the First Emperor of Qin) and established a feudal bureaucratic system, promulgated county administrations, standardized weights, money, Chinese characters and built the Great Wall and "highways". The initiatives benefited the united country and promoted development of the economy. But the First Emperor did some autocratic acts such as burning books and killing scholars, using a large conscripted labour force to construct the Afang Palace and his mausoleum, levying heavy rents and taxes and issuing cruel laws, which damaged production and hindered progress in society. The first national uprising of peasants in Chinese

history occurred soon after his death.

ARCHAEOLOGICAL RELICS OF QIN SHIHUANG'S STANDARDIZATION OF WEIGHTS, MONEY AND CHINESE CHARACTERS

The Qin Kingdom had an internal reform of the system of weights and measures during Shang Yang's Reform in 356 B. C. and later kings attached importance to the settled system. When Ying Zheng came to power, he had the weights and measures checked twice each year, in February and August. After the unification of the six states, he carried out a series of measures to strengthen the united country and develop the economy, and standardizing of weights and measures was one of them. A copper plate carrying the imperial edict was unearthed from the Xianyang area in November 1961. The plate is 9.9 cm. long, 6.2 cm. wide and 0.2 cm. thick and there is a nail hole in each of the four corners. The plate might have been fastened to a wooden measure but fell off when the wooden measure rotted. The imperial edict read, "Year 26, the Emperor has defeated all dukes and annexed the whole land. The whole land under the sky is at peace and the First Emperor has been entitled. The Prime Minister is sent to check the weights and measures and this measure is authorized".

About 20 weights and measures have been found and there are two kinds of measures: made of copper or clay in the shape

2 - 3   Imperial edict of Qin

2 - 4 Bronze oval - shaped measure with inscriptions of Qin

of a square or an oval. The container of measures had: one
sheng, two sheng, two and a half sheng, four sheng, half dou
(five sheng) and two dou. The system of weights in the Qin
Dynasty is that one jin equals 256. 25 grams. In the Qin
Dynasty the strict system of weights and measures was used
mainly for easy collecting of rent and tax and distributing their
salary to officials. But it was helpful for the exchange of goods
in the market and promoted business activities impartially.

There were various kinds of money in the Spring and
Autumn Period (770 to 476 B. C.) and during Warring States
times (475 B. C. to 221 B. C.) because each state had its own
monetary system. After unifying China, the First Emperor

issued a law standardizing the monetary system. It abolished such forms of money as pearl, jade, shell, silver, tin and other copper coins. The copper coin was the main money issued and its face value was designed to meet the need of exchange. The shape of the copper coin was round with a square hole in the middle according to a theory that "the sky is round and the earth is square". The copper coin was the earliest standardized money and replaced money in the shape of a knife, spade, cloth and others shapes. The "round and square" shape went largely unchanged as the national standard of money over the last 2,000 years of feudal society.

2 - 5   "Ban Liang" bronze coin of Qin

In order to maintain the value of the official money and protect it from inflation, the First Emperor decreed that the minting of coins was the preserve of the government alone and the private manufacture of coins was forbidden. Violators

2 - 6   Inscriptions on stone in Zeshan Mountain (rubbing)

would be punished severely.

Before Qin Shihuang, the written script (calligraphy) was called a large seal style. After unifying the country he standardized the script into the small seal style and used it as the official calligraphy. The First Emperor led his officials on tours of inspection throughout China. Wherever he went, stone tablets with carved inscriptions were set up to memorialize the

Emperor's achievements. Many tablets about the First Emperor's tour of inspection to the east were damaged or lost. Only two inscribed tablets "the Taishan Carved Stone" and "the Langye Carved Stone" have survived. The calligraphy was traditionally attributed to the hand of Prime Minister Li Si.

At the same time, the calligraphy in daily use during the Qin Dynasty was not like the standard small seal character of the stone inscriptions, but rather was square seal character similar to the late official script. So there were three styles of calligraphy in the Qin Dynasty: the large seal style, the small seal style and the official style with them being able to be divided into carved characters and written characters. The carved characters were found in the garden of Qin Shihuang's Mausoleum. They were not attributed to the hands of calligraphers but the hands of ordinary people. They implied realty of calligraphy of the Qin Dynasty more really.

BUILDING OF THE GREAT WALL
AND THE EARLIEST HIGHWAYS

In late Warring States times (475 to 221 B.C.) the Yan, Zhao and Qin states, which shared borders with the Hu Nation, individually built great walls to defend themselves against the Hu, but the walls were not linked. In 222 B.C. when the Qin was attacking the State of Yan in the north (after conquering the State of Zhao), the Hu Nation took the chance to occupy the former territory of the Zhao. After defeating the six states, Qin Shihuang ordered his general Meng Tian to lead 300,000 troops to win back the land. To resist aggression from the Hu Nation, Qin Shihuang had the Great Wall built. The former walls built by Zhao, Yan and Qin were linked and solidified and extended to the north following the topography. The builders of the Great Wall were General Meng Tian's 300,000 troops and labourers, prisoners and other captives. Food and building materials supplied by internal counties flowed like water to the building sites. It took tens of years to complete the Great Wall which stretched 5,500 km from Lin Tao in the west to Liao Dong in the east. Both the Great Wall and Qin Mausoleum were placed on the list of the world's heritage protection in December 1989.

The highways to the whole country built in the First Emperor's time were also miracles in the history of construction. During the Spring and Autumn Period (770 to 476 B.C.) and Warring States times (475 to 221 B.C.), each state built walls, dams and trenches at its boundaries for defence against the others. These works inhibited transportation and after unification the First Emperor ordered them to be removed.

About a million soldiers and labourers were called up to build roads on an unprecedented scale. The roads were of four types: 1) "racing roads" for the Emperor's chariots; 2) straight roads mainly for the use of a war; 3) new roads in the

2 - 7   The Great Wall

southern part of China and 4) "five chi (A measurement, one chi is equal to 0.3 metres.) roads" in west – southern part of China. The "racing roads" were 50 steps wide and trees were planted every 10 metres on both sides. Of the remainder of the roads archeological study has found that the middle was higher than the sides to drain water easily and the surface was rammed with steel tools. By using an advanced technology of geographical survey a straight road was built from Xianyang, the Qin capital, to Jiu Yuan (now Baotou, Inner Mongolia) for the First Emperor to transport troops and military supplies to the frontier quickly.

Chinese roads and highways have developed continuously

2 - 8   Remains of a straight highway

since the Qin Dynasty, but some were discarded and ruined. However, from their layout and basic form, the roads of the Qin Dynasty roughly created the basic structure of transportation in China over the last 2,000 years.

The roads built in the First Emperor's time, with the Capital Xianyang as the centre and stretching to the whole country, not only strengthened the central government's control of regional governments, but also facilitated the exchange of economy and culture and promoted the unity of the Chinese nations.

III. XIANYANG – A FAMOUS WORLD METROPOLIS IN THE 3RD CENTURY B.C.

Xianyang was the capital of the Qin Kingdom 2,350 years ago, but the city name.

"Xianyang", had not been used before. The Xianyang area was under the administration of Yongzhou in the Xia Dynasty (about 21st – 16th century B.C.) and a kingdom named "Biguo" was set up there during the Shang Dynasty (16th – 11th century B.C.) and the Zhou Dynasty (11th century – 256 B.C.). When Feng and later Gao (near present day Xi'an) were made the capital in the Zhou Dynasty, Xianyang being near both cities was their environs. A peasant uprising against the Zhou Dynasty occurred in 770 B.C. and King Zhou Ping fled accompanied by Duke Qin Xiang. Duke Qin Xiang was granted land to the west of Xianyang because of his assistance to King Zhou Ping. Xianyang was located between the Wei River and a mountain. Ancient people called a place north of a river or south of a mountain as "Yang" meaning receiving more sunshine. "Xian" means double. Xianyang is located on the northern bank of the Wei River and the southern part of Mount Jiuzong and so the name means

3 - 1   Marks of craftsmen on the terra - cotta
figures (rubbing)

"double sunshine". Xianyang was the capital of the Qin
Kingdom, as well as a capital of ancient China later.

THE QIN CAPITAL MOVED TO XIANYANG

Qin Xiang was granted a piece of land and the title of "Duke" to establish his kingdom in 770 B.C.. The Qin people then fought the Rong and Di nations for over 100 years eventually defeating them and occupying the whole Wei River Valley including Xianyang City.

3-2　Roof tile-end with animals design

The Qin Kingdom had been located in the wilderness and its economy was weak and slow to develop. It was looked down on by other kingdoms in the early stage of its establishment.

But the Qin Kingdom developed rapidly after it occupied the Wei River Valley. Thanks to fertile conditions and the influence of the traditional agriculture of the former Zhou people, its agricultural production expanded and surpassed the output of its own husbandry.

3 - 3   Bronze tripod Inlaid with gold and silver

The Qin persisted in pushing eastwards after Duke Qin Mao (659 - 621 B. C.) had begun to enlarge his kingdom. After 400 years of hard fighting the Qin people settled down in the central of China. The Qin Kingdom became one of the kingdoms of the Zhou Dynasty and it linked the central government and nations in the northwest regions together.

Compared with other states in central China, the Qin was later in carrying out reform, but its reform was successful.

3 – 4   Model of palace No. 1 of Xianyang

Duke Qin Xiao (361 – 338 B. C.) entrusted his Prime Minister, Shang Yang, to carry out the first reform in 339 B. C. It lasted 10 years and achieved good results and the Qin were strengthened. Shang Yang began his second reform in 350 B. C. and moved the Qin Capital to Xianyang from Leyang (east of present Xi'an). Xianyang was considered a strategic location because of its position between the Wei and Jing Rivers, and on a route for attack of the other six kingdoms in the east. Shang Yang was appointed a supervisor in the building of the Capital.

Chinese history showed that it was from Xianyang that Shang Yang published his reforms and it was from Xianyang that the Qin started to attack other kingdoms. Xianyang was an active city in the east in 4th − 3rd Century B.C..

XIANYANG BEFORE THE UNIFICATION OF CHINA

When Shang Yang supervised the construction of Capital Xianyang, palaces were built with gate towers. The gate tower was a symbol of power of the Court. A site of a construction base was found 15 km. northeast of present Xianyang. It is 8 metres high above the ground and there are 400 metres between two gate towers. The long distance between the gate towers show how large and great were the palaces, which those of

3 − 5   Rubbing from a Hollow Brick with dragon design

other kingdoms could not compare. The western gate tower w as excavated and found by testing that it had been built around

3 - 6   door ornament from the Qin's palace

340 B. C. It had three stories with an attic on the top floor. It was the first time gate towers and a palace were combined, having living quarters and offices of the emperor, forming an above - ground construction.

Since the Qin moved its capital to Xianyang, King Hui Wen, King Dao Wu, King Zhao Xiang, King Xiao Wen and King Zhuang Xiang ruled there for around 120 years. During that period, construction and enlarging of Xianyang occurred, and it became the largest city in China. A large number of palaces were scattered around the Xianyang area when Qin Shihuang came to the throne in 238 B. C. .

When Qin Shihuang was conquering other states and unifying China, "he had palaces copying those of another state

3 - 7   Mural of a chariot and four horses from the Qin's palace

set up in the Xianyang area after defeating that state. There were a lot of palaces and constructions with characteristics of other states" (reported in the "Record of the Historian" by Sima Qian, the great early historian in 100 B. C.). Archaeological studies have found many remaining sites of former constructions on the northern plateau of present day Xianyang. They were of different designs with different layouts and must have been thecopies of palaces of other states.

Prince Ying Zheng (later Qin Shihuang) inherited the throne at the age of 13 after King Zhuang Xiang died in 238 B. C.. His godfather, Lu Buwei administrated the state for him. After 9 years, Ying Zheng assumed power at 22. He went to war with other states from the base of Xianyang and conquered the states of Chu, Qi, Yan, Han, Zhao, Wei one after another from 230 B. C. to 221 B. C.. Ying Zheng became the first Emperor of unified China and he ascended the throne as the First Emperor of China in Xianyang. He established a feudal political system and standardized weights and measures, the monetary system and the system of written Chinese characters. The Qin people were very happy after the unification of China.

XIANYANG AFTER THE UNIFICATION OF CHINA

After Qin Shihuang unified China, Xianyang was the capital of China. The First Emperor ordered enlarging the scale of the city for the reason that "more people live in Xianyang and the former palaces are too small" (said in the "Record of the Historian" by Sima Qian). More new palaces were built with Xianyang Palace as the centre. Many palaces, pavilions, towers and offices were scattered over an area of 25,000 sq. km. from Chunhua in the north and Huxian in the south, Qianshui in the west and the Yellow River in the east. 270 palaces and towers around Xianyang Palace covered 100 square km. Each palace or tower was linked by straight ways. The "San Po Huang Tu", by Chen Zhi in the Tang Dynasty, said that "all the palaces, buildings and towers like stars in the sky were set up along the Wei River which was considered as the Milky Way according to the theory of astronomical phenomena". The design of the construction implied that the Qin people considered themselves at the centre on the earth.

Many palaces such as Xianyang Palace, Xin Palace, Afang Palace were built and among them Afang Palace was the largest and most magnificent.

3 – 8   Museum of the Qin's palace

The group of palaces around Xianyang City was great and marvelous, and Xianyang's trade and culture prospered and transportation was very convenient. There had been straight ways from Xianyang to Inner Mongolia in the north before the unification and "many ways were built with Xianyang as the centre to radiating faraway places". The historical book "Han Book" said that "Highways from Xianyang stretched to Yan and Qi in the east, to Wu and Chu in the south and far to the ocean in the Qin dynasty. The highways were 50 steps wide and pine trees were planted along the edges. The convenience of transportation brought about the rapid development of commerce. The Chinese characters "亭" (ting) and "里" (li) found in pottery excavated in the Xianyang area showed that Xianyang had a strict administrative system and market management system. From archaeological materials it can be analyzed that there were palace districts, residential areas, or workshops districts. There were some wealthy families or business persons such as Zhuo, Wushi Ke, and Widow Qing in Xianyang. The population in Xianyang was 7 - 800,000 at that time. Qin art was unique in Chinese history and implies the style of magnificence and beauty. As the capital city, there lived great artists and masters in Xianyang and various art masterpieces were made there. From the pottery Chinese characters "宫彊" (Gong jiang), "宫保" (Gong bao), "咸阳衣" (Xianyang yi), "咸阳亲" (Xianyang Qin) found in the terra-cotta figures, it could be shown that the makers of the figures were masters and most of them came from pottery workshops of the court in Xianyang or they were famous Xianyang artists. Xianyang was not only the capital of the Qin Dynasty - the first of unified China, but also a famous world metropolis in the third century B.C.. Its influence on Oriental culture was as strong as that of the Greek and Roman's on western culture.

After Qin Shihuang unified China, 12,000 royal or wealthy families of the six former states were forced to move to the Xianyang area because Qin Shihuang wished to cut their links with their former states.

To strengthen his authority, the Fist Emperor ordered the collection of all weapons from the former six states and their royal families in 213 B.C. The weapons were melted down and cast into 12 statues standing in front of Afang palace. In the same year Confucian scholars criticized the Court and Qin Shiuhaung adopted cruel methods against them. He ordered their books be burnt and in the following year 460 Confucian scholars were captured and buried alive. This was a great tragedy of culture in Chinese history.

Xianyang was the city where the Qin carried out its reform, developed, and began to unify China, but it was also the place where the Qin was defeated. Xianyang, as the Capital of the Qin and then China, lasted 144 years. "Afang Poem" said "it was the Qin who conquered six states but it was not the six states which finally defeated Qin (meaning the Qin was defeated by itself)".

General Xiang Yu led his troops to attack Xianyang City and occupied it in 206 B. C.. They set fire to the palaces and the fires lasted 3 days and magnificent Xianyang City was burnt down and left in ruins. People today feel regretful about this.

The archaeological exploration and excavation of ancient Xianyang began in the 1950s and about 230 historical sites have been found and 6 of them excavated. The excavated area covers about 15,000 square metres and over 100 tombs of Qin have been found. More than 5,000 pieces of relics have been unearthed and collected. But it is still difficult to draw an outline of ancient Xianyang City from the historical records and the archaeological studies to date.

According to the investigations, ancient Xianyang was located between the Wei River in the south and the Jing River to the north. No remains of the city wall have been discovered, but some remains of a base of a wall have been found in the east of present Xianyang. The northern wall was calculated to be 843 metres long, the western wall 576 metres long , the southern wall 902 metres long, but the remains of eastern wall base have not been found. The wall formed an oblong shape. Some pieces of pottery and tile were discovered on the remains of the northern wall base which was 5.5 - 7.6 metres wide. It has been inferred that it was a palace wall built in the Warring States Period (475 - 221 B.C.).

Remains of 20 rammed foundation bases were found in ancient Xianyang City and 8 are located within the palace walls. Three of the 8 were excavated. The No.1 foundation base was an elevated platform with rooms around the rammed - earth base. These were living rooms, sitting rooms and bathrooms. In the middle of the platform there was a main palace hall. All the rooms were separated with rammed earth, or earthen bricks. There were corridors around the main palace hall and around the rooms at the ground level. There were also drainage ditches on both levels. The No.2 Base was located to the northeast of the No.1 and as the No.1 it was an elevated construction. 5 remains of palace rooms were found on the top of the platform and the 4th room was a main hall. There were remains of a basement and underground rooms and corridors also. The former main structure is unclear from the No. 3 remains, but there is evidence of 11 rooms around the platform. During the excavation, large amounts of building materials were unearthed and they included round tiles, plate tiles, tile ends, paving bricks, hollow bricks and remains of rotten wood, bamboo and mats. In addition some pottery vessels, small bronze figures and remnants of murals were unearthed. The murals showed people, animals, plant, buildings and goat figures. The drawing methods were strong and rough, careful but not too complicated. The colors were red, black, white, red and were made from minerals. Besides the above mentioned items, some pieces of clothing and rough silk were found and all are treasures for the archaeological study of Qin history.

The remains of the ancient Xianyang city wall have not been found and it might be that the Wei River moved northwards and flooded the southern wall, or for some other reason. It is still unknown how large was ancient Xianyang. The excavated remains of Xianyang City were listed as a National Protection Sites of Cultural Relics by the State Council of China in January 1988 and the Museum of the Xianyang Palace Remains was established and opened to public in 1995. The Museum, covering an area of 0.7 hectares, is located beside the remains of Xianyang Palace 10 km northeast of present day Xianyang.

When Liu Bang overthrew the Qin Dynasty and established the Han Dynasty, he moved his capital to Chang'an City (present day Xi'an) which was not far from ancient Xianyang.

IV. QIN SHIHUANG'S E'PANG PALACE AND ITS GOLDEN STATUES

E'Pang Palace was one of the famous palaces in the ancient city of Xianyang. It was built on the southern bank of the Wei River when King Hui Wen of the Qin Kingdom was in power, but the project came to a stop when he died. After Qin

4-1   The section of the tamped earthen platform of the front hall
of E'Pang Palace

Shihuang unified China, he ordered 700,000 people to rebuild and enlarge E'Pang Palace. However, the project was too large to be completed before Qin Shihuang's death. The Second

Emperor of Qin continued the project after his father's death. But it was not fully completed until the end of the Qin Dynasty. In the "Recorder of the Grand Historian" by Sima Qian (the great early historian in 100 B. C) itis said that the front hall of the palace was 500 steps long from east to west and 500 chi (170 metres) wide from north to south. It could hold 10,000 people. There were paved roadways from the Palace to a mountain to the south and to Xianyang in the north across the Wei River. Du Mu, a famous poet in the Tang Dynasty (618 – 907), wrote about Afang Palace in a poem, "Leaving Mount Shu, Afang Palace can be seen. All the palaces stretched over a distance of 300 li (150 km.) and there are many towers and pavilions between the palaces. " From this description it can be imagined how great and magnificent was the view of Afang Palace.

WHY WAS IT CALLED E'PANG PALACE?

It is a pity that the magnificent palace group was burned. The ruins were located in the western suburbs of Xi'an City and an elevated earthen platform and some remains of constructional materials could be seen. The remains were listed as National Protection Sites of cultural relics in 1961. Archaeological workers found dozens of Qin construction ruins and two of them are clear. One is a large rammed – earth base, 20 metres high and 31 metres in circumference. The other is an

4 − 2   Roof tile − end with 12 Chinese characters

oblong shaped elevated earthen base which is 7 metres high and 1,300 metres long from east to west and 500 metres wide from north to south. The total area of the base is about 650,000 square metres. The base was larger than the front hall of palace described in "Recorder of the Grand Historian" by Sima Qian and it might be the base of the front hall, corridors, steps and other auxiliary constructions. Many plate tiles, round tiles, hollow bricks with pattern designs, pottery drainage pipes, brazen constructional joints and others have been unearthed.

"E' Pang" was not a usual formal name for a palace in ancient China and so the name of "E'Pang" has attracted a lot of attention later. Chinese "Fang" means "house", but there is no meaning for "A" alone. People wondered why the palace

4-3   Bronze Weight with Inscriptions "高奴禾石"

was called "Afang" and what it meant. In "Recorder of the Grand Historian" it is said "Afang Palace was not completed. A formal name would be given after it had been built. Local people called a palace 'a house' so people later called it E'Pang Palace. But there are other explanations. One said that E'Pang meant high, the name being given because the palace was set on a high platform. Another saying was that E'Pang meant large and wide, the name being given because the front hall of the palace (which was completed) was very large and wide. But all considered that the name "E'Pang" was a temporary name because it wasn't finished. However, there was another explanation which thought "Er" meant near, the name being given because the palace was near Xianyang. Who knows which saying is right?

12 GOLDEN STATUES

Li Bai, a famous poet during the Tang Dynasty (618 – 907) wrote a poem, "Emperor Qin Defeated Six Kingdoms" which described the situation at the time. At the end of the Warring States Period (475 – 221 B. C.) there were many wars in China. Qin Shihuang led his strong troops and conquered the other six kingdoms from 234 to 221 B. C. . After he defeated a kingdom, he ordered a copy of its palace to be built in the Xianyang area. Royal families of the kingdoms were forced to move to Xianyang. After his unification of China, all weapons from the six kingdoms and royal and wealthy families were collected and melted down and cast into 12 golden statues. The 12 statues implied the power and honour of the Qin Imperial rule. They were standing in front of E'Pang Palace along its approach and added a great magnificent view to the palace.

The 12 "golden" statues were not really made of gold because golden weapons have never been found in archaeological excavations. It was said in the historical book "San Po Huang Tu" that each statue weighted 34,000 jin – about 3075 kg. How could they mine and smelt such a weight of gold at that time? The statues were in fact made of bronze. Ancient people called bronze "gold" so the bronze statues were called "golden statues".

4 – 4   The simulated scene of Kingdom Qin'palace

Why did Qin Shihuang have the "golden statues" cast? It remains a mystery. A historical book of the Han Dynasty (206 B.C. – 220 AD) said that 12 giants wearing clothes of the Yi nation once walked the streets of Xianyang City and soon disappeared when the Qin had conquered the six kingdoms. The giants were around 17 metres tall and very strong. Qin Shihuang thought them to be lucky symbols and so ordered the casting of "golden statues" modeled on these 12 giants. They all stood in front of E'Pang Palace after they were cast. But there was second explanation. Ruan Wuzhong was a great general from South China and he was 4 metres tall and very strong and powerful. He was ordered by Qin Shihuang to conquer Lintiao (a strategical place) which he did successfully.

He was loyal to Qin Shihuang and fought the enemy bravely. After his death, Qin Shihuang ordered a statue of him be cast and stand outside E'Pang Palace in order to commemorate him and encourage other generals and officials to be loyal to the court and fight bravely. However, there was the third saying that seems reasonable. Qin Shihuang collected all the weapons and had them melted down and cast into statues for he want to strengthen his authority. He didn't want the weapons to remain with the people and be a threat. He cast them into statues to show his authority.

The golden statues were huge and it was said each was about 17 metres tall and its pedestal was 10 metres tall. On the pedestals there were descriptions written by Prime Minister Li Si and Meng Tian, a Qin general. The pedestals were hollow and there was a machine inside each linking them together. The 12 statues could turn around and make different music when the machines worked.

WHERE HAVE THE 12 GOLDEN STATUES GONE?

Where have the 12 golden statues gone? The 12 golden statues originally stood in front of Afang Palace. They were moved to the front of Changle Palace after Liu Bang overthrew the Qin Dynasty and established the Han Dynasty (206 B. C. – 220 AD). Wang Mang, a general of the Western Han overthrew the then Emperor in 8 A. D and proclaimed himself

Emperor. He was ill at ease and at a night dreamed that the golden statues became alive. He considered it a bad omen and ordered people to damage the descriptions on the pedestals. When Emperor Xian of Han Dynasty was in power later, the economy of the society was very poor and the court had financial problems. So the Emperor ordered 10 of the golden statues to be melted down and cast into coins. The other 2 statues were laid down in a storage building. Cai Run, Emperor Ming of the Wei Kingdom (220 – 265 A. D.) set up his capital in Leyang (Leyang City, Henan Province now) in 237. He ordered all the symbols of former Emperors to be collected at Leyang. He planned to move the 2 statues to Leyang. But the statues were too heavy and after attempting to remove them from Chang'an City they were left in Banqiao (eastern suburbs of Xi'an city now).

Over 100 years later, Shi Jilong of the Later Zhao Kingdom established his capital in Yecheng (in present Hebei Province) and the 2 statues were carried to Yecheng. But they were removed to Chang'an by the Former Qin Kingdom after it occupied Yecheng in 370. The 2 statues were melted down and cast into coins in Chang'an City some time later.

The statues survived about 600 years and their technology and art value were of a very high standard. They showed a unique capacity of creation and wisdom of the ancient Chinese in being able to make such huge statues over 2000 years ago.

In the late of 1980's a reproduction palace was built in the

4 - 5   The simulated scene of the front hall of E'Pang Palace

southern Xi'an as a movie set for the feature film "Emperor Qin Shihuang". It was a composite reproduction combining features from a number of Qin palaces. In front of this reproduction of Emperor Qin's Palace there now stand 12 gilded golden statues which are replicas of the former 12 golden statues. However, they are not as tall as the originals and they are not made of bronze, but of modern metallic materials. People can imagine the sight of the former 12 golden statues when they see the modern replicas.

V. THE GREATEST SECRET OF THE QIN DYNASTY IS BURIED IN THE QIN MAUSOLEUM

Qin Shihuang wished to live forever and searched for miraculous medicines to lengthen his life. He disliked talking about death, but he knew that no one could break the laws of nature. He attempted to move his earthly empire to heaven and establish an underground empire that was as glorious as the one he ruled over when alive. This was the reason he built such a magnificent mausoleum.

Qin Shihuang died at age of 50 in Autumn 210 B.C. and was buried in his mausoleum.

WHY DID QIN SHIHUANG CHOOSE LISHAN MOUNTAIN AS HIS BURIAL PLACE

Lishan Mountain is an extinct volcano and there are many hot springs. The temperature of water flowing out of the ground reaches 43 centigrade and the water contains minerals such as sodium carbonate, and has effects of curing skin diseases.

There are several reasons for Qin Shihuang to choose

Lishan Mountain as his burial place. From the point of view of a geomagnetic omen the place was ideal with mountains in the south and the Wei River in the north. His back laid against the mountain and feet pointed to the river. Also the tombs of Qin Shihuang's ancestors were located in Ziyang, west of Lintong. As a descendant he should have his tomb east of Ziyang. It was then a rule that later generations were buried to the east of their older ones.

Chinese emperors usually gave names to their tombs in ancient times. What was the name of the Qin mausoleum? A bronze vessel unearthed from the east of the mausoleum had words carved in it reading "Lishan Garden, containing 12 dou and weight 2 jun and 13 jin". This means that the mausoleum was named "Lishan Garden". But a historical book said it was called "Mount Lishan". Some historians and experts argue it was named "Qin Mausoleum" as people called other tombs of the emperors. There is still not agreement.

THE ARCHAEOLOGICAL DISCOVERIES IN THE QIN SHIHUANG MAUSOLEUM

Archaeological studies of the "Qin Mausoleum Garden" started as early as the 1930s. The Historical Academy of Beiping Institute sent people to search fields of Shaanxi Province and collect materials of the Qin culture. Archaeological workers began a ground investigation in the mausoleum area in the 1950s and the Qin Mausoleum Garden was listed as a key unit under the national protection by the State Council in 1960.

But the archaeological study stopped and the Mausoleum Garden was poorly protected in late '60s and early '70s. Lan Anwen, a reporter at the Beijing – based News Agency wrote a report in 1974 entitled "Terra – cotta Warriors of the Qin Dynasty Unearthed in the Tomb Area of the First Emperor" in which he wrote, "The Qin Mausoleum is an important unit under the national protection, but is not well protected. Farmers take earth from the tomb area and grow crops there. Pottery fragments and copper artifacts have been unearthed, but thrown around." The report attracted the attention of high leaders in the Central Government. As the terra – cotta figures became known to the public a planned archaeological research and excavation program has been established in the whole tomb area since 1974.

At the time of writing around 600 various sized burial pits and attendant tombs and around a million square metres of ruins of ground constructions have been found and 50,000 artifacts unearthed. The exploration is continuing and new discoveries will be made. The excavations now include the vaults of the terra-cotta warriors and horses to the east of the mausoleum, the two bronze chariots to the west of the mausoleum, the ruins of funerary buildings and houses to the north and west of the tumulus, the ruins of horse pens and a vault of rare birds and animals, the ruins of a fishing pool, a ruin of a stone – material processing site, attendants' tombs in Shi Jiao village and a graveyard of mausoleum builders. They are all invaluable for study by experts of government policy, the military, folk customs and the material and cultural lives of people in the Qin Dynasty.

RUINS OF GROUND CONSTRUCTIONS DISCOVERED IN THE QIN MAUSOLEUM GARDEN

According to archaeological exploration and excavation the Qin mausoleum covers an area of 56.25 square kilometers and was enclosed by two city walls – the inner and outer walls. The inner wall measured 1,355 metres in length from north to south and 580 metres in width from east to west, with a circumference of 3,870 metres long. A partition wall in the middle of the inner city divided them into two – the northern and southern parts. Further, a wall in the northern part divided it into two – the eastern and western zones. The tumulus, in the shape of a square pyramid, lies in the southern part and has three steps in its profile. After 2,200 years of erosion by rain and wind and damage by man the tumulus is now 87 metres high and its base is 350 metres in length from north to south and 345 metres in width from east to west.

The outer city wall was 2,165 metres long from north to south, 940 metres wide from east to west with a circumference

5 – 1   Pottery drain pipe unearthed from the Qin mausoleum garden

of 6,210 metres long. There were gates in the inner city wall
and the outer city wall facing in four directions. There were 6
gates in the inner city while there was four gates in the outer
city. At each gate there was a construction called the gate
building.

A part of the south wall of the inner grounds measuring
one to three metres high remains, but of the rest there is only
the ruins of the wall base. The wall base was about 8 metres
wide.

Many ruins of constructions were discovered between the
inner grounds and the outer grounds. Among them are the

5 - 2   A roof tile - end found in the Qin mausoleam gorden

ruins of the funeral building and its accessory building which were found 40 metres from the north of the tumulus. The buildings were used for holding memorial ceremonies. A lot of building materials, iron tools and pottery artifact fragments were unearthed from the ruins covering an area of 3,575 square metres.

In the south - western part, between the inner grounds and the outer grounds, three ruins of building bases were discovered and many pottery fragments having some carved characters were unearthed. The experts say there is no doubt the ruins are of the houses in which the officials lived who were in charge of food and memorial ceremony in the Mausoleum

Garden.

　　Besides the above, the ruins of a dam was discovered to the south of the tumulus. The dam protected the mausoleum from flood water rushing out of the valley of Lishan Mountain. The ruins of houses, where the supervisors lived, were discovered 1,300 metres north of the tumulus and also to the east and west of the vaults of the Entombed Warriors. Ruins of sheds where the workers, who made the terra－cotta figures and horses, lived were found too.

VI. SECRETS OF THE UNDERGROUND PALACE OF THE QIN MAUSOLEUM

The discoveries of the vaults of the terra-cotta figures, the pits of the bronze chariots, the stone armour vaults and other attendant tombs shook the world. Now more and more people are turning their attention to the underground palace of the Qin Mausoleum.

WHERE IS THE UNDERGROUND PALACE?

The underground palace lies beneath the Qin tumulus and was built as "an underground heaven". The underground palace is about 30 metres below ground level and has doors facing in four directions, 5 doors to the east and one each in the three other compass directions.

The details of the underground construction are unknown, but the "Historical Records" (written by Sima Qian in 100 B. C.) described it so: "As soon as he became king of the Qin State, construction of his tomb was started at Lishan Mountain, and after he unified the country over 700, 000 conscripts from all parts of the country were summoned to work there. They dug through the subterranean streams and poured

6 - 1   Tumulus(earthen burial mound)of the Qin First Emperor

molten copper for the outer coffin. The tomb was filled with models of palaces, pavilions and offices, fine vessels, precious stones and rarities. Artisans were ordered to set-up crossbows in the tomb so that any thief breaking in would be shot dead. There is a map of the sky on the ceiling and a topographical map on the floor with circulating mercury to represent the waters of the earth. Eternal lamps were lit with man - fish grease (allegedly taken from a kind of four - legged and human - looking fish living in the East China Sea)."

We are uncertain about the truth of the description, but a geophysical survey in the 1980s determined that there was in fact an area of 12, 000 square metres of unnatural concentrations of mercury in the area under the tumulus.

Archaeological research implies that the top of the palace was square shaped and 2.7 to 4 metres below ground level. The palace is 392 metres wide from east to west, 460 metres from north to south with a total area of 180,320 square metres. There is not another tomb in the world, which can compare with such a large tomb chamber as the underground palace. The walls of the palace were 4 metres high and 4 metres wide, and were made of unbaked bricks. There were five doors facing east and one in the other three directions. The room with the coffin was called the inner chamber. It was the core of the palace and no doubt was located in the very center.

WHAT IS IN THE UNDERGROUND PALACE?

In 1981 and 1982 experts employed a scientific method of detection for determining the presence of mercury and found that a mercury deviation did exist in the rammed soil near the mausoleum. The area of mercury deviation covered 12,000 square metres and it verified the records about mercury in the tomb written by Sima Qian.

"A topographical map on the floor with circulating mercury to represent the waters of the earth" means that rivers were modeled with mercury and, by some mechanical means, made to flow into a miniature ocean. That "The tomb was filled with models of palaces, pavilions and offices, fine vessels, precious stones and rarities" implies the underground palace was built as a replica of the real palace in which the Qin First Emperor lived.

6 - 2   Luxurious coffin unearthed from a tomb of West Han
          Dynasty (in Dabaotai, Beijing)

WHY HAS THE UNDERGROUND PALACE NOT BEEN OPENED?

Natural damage and destruction of cultural relics has been shocking and distressful. A Chu tomb of Warring States times (475 to 221 B. C.) was excavated in Xianyang, Henan Province, in 1957 and when the tomb was opened, piles of bamboo strips with Chinese characters were found in liquid. However the bamboo strips began to roll up and became black and the characters disappeared soon after workers removed them from the liquid and put them on a table for photographing. Mawangdui tomb of the Han Dynasty (25 to 220 A.D.) was excavated in the Changsha, Hunan Province, in the early 1970s. To everyone's surprise, the corpse was in good condition and burial peaches and other fruit were fresh when they were found. But the burial peaches and fruit turned to water in a few minutes before being photographed. The corpse dried out when it was taken from the tomb.

When the late Premier Zhou Enlai visited Shaanxi Province for an inspection in the early 1960s, the Shaanxi Provincial Government put forward a proposal to excavate the Qianling mausoleum of the Tang Dynasty (618 to 907). But it was not approved and Premier Zhou quipped humorously "We still haven't a scientific technique of protecting unearthed cultural relics from destruction. Let the Earth God protect the remains, left by our ancestors for us, for further years".

There is currently not an effective technology in the world to protect unearthed organic cultural relics.

Around 25 years have passed since the Entombed Warriors began to be excavated in 1974. However, initially damage to them surpassed imagination. When the terra－cotta figures were unearthed some of them were colourful, but the colour fell off, or faded, after a few days. The metal weapons oxidized when exposed to air. After efforts over many years, experts in cultural preservation both in China and abroad, have devised a method to preserve the colour on the terra－cotta figures and horses.

If the underground palace is excavated, more treasures will be found. However, it is very difficult to protect such treasures from natural destruction.

Apart from preservation techniques, experts have pointed out four other problems:

1) The underground palace covers an area of 180,320 square metres and a permanent covering should be set up to protect the palace from erosion by rain as it is excavated. A square shaped protective covering should have a span of, at least, 500 metres, but there isn't presently such a large structure in the world.

2) There is a lot of underground water in the mausoleum area and water can be found only 16 metres below ground level. Most of the palace constructions are below 16 metres. Without large pumps to pump out water as excavations occur, the whole palace would be inundated.

3) The rammed earth in and under the tumulus is about a hundred thick. It is not easy to move the earth away.

4) Mercury concentrations beneath the tumulus are 280 times higher than normal levels and are harmful to humans. It is a major task how to treat it. Also other unforeseeable difficulties will be met when the mausoleum is excavated.

In other words, major difficulties remain for excavation of the Qin mausoleum at present.

VII. THE FATE OF
QIN SHIHUANG'S CHILDREN

In the history of ancient China there were numerous tragedies where princes of the imperial families killed each other to gain control of the throne.

HOW MANY CHILDREN DID QIN SHIHUANG HAVE?

Qin Shihuang had an empress, many concubines and maids, and of course many children. There was no clear historical record of how many children he had. But we can gain some insights from indirect records. "Historical Records & Biography of Li Si" (a part of the "Historical Records" that was written by Sima Qian) says, "Shihuang's tenth daughter Tuo died in Duo (a place)". From this we know Qin Shihuang had at least ten daughters. "Historical Records" say "Qin Shihuang had 12 princes." And another historical book recorded, "Shihuang has over 20 sons". "Notes of Collection", an attached book of "Historical Records", says, "After the Qin First Emperor died, Li Si dethroned the 17th son and made the now Emperor his successor". From the records, we can deduce Qin Shihuang had over 20 sons.

A historical book "The Collective Pictures of Old and Today" stated that when Qin Shihuang went hunting and stayed at Shuntian, his young son died and was buried at Duanti Village 30 km north of the city. In the "Historical Records of Shandong Province", recorded when Qin Shihuang went to inspect in the north of Qufu County, it is said his daughter died and was buried there.

In other historical records about Qin Shihuang's activities, it is mentioned that his eldest son Fu Su was once a supervisor in General Meng Tian's army.

From a study of many historical books, only a few names of his sons and daughters were found. They were the eldest son Fu Su, a young son Hu Hai (the Second Emperor), Prince Gao, Prince Jiang and Princess Hua Yang.

THE TRAGEDY OF QIN SHIHUANG'S CHILDREN

Qin Shihuang went on an Inspection Tour of his realm in 210 B. C. and the request of his young son Hu Hai to follow was approved. Qin Shihuang died of an illness at Pingtai (Pingxiang County, now Hebei Province) and Hu Hai was the only son present. A high official Zhao Gao devised a conspiracy and he, Hu Hai, and the Prime Minister Li Si formed an alliance. They went against Qin Shihuang's dying edict and promulgated another saying Hu Hai was chosen by the Emperor to succeed him on the throne and that Fu Su, the eldest son was ordered to commit suicide. When they reached the Capital and showed the forged edict to Fu Su (who should have succeeded to the throne) he cried out and committed suicide before establishing whether the edict was true, or not.

Hu Hai became the Second Emperor by conspiratorial means, but he was not at ease. Zhao Gao proposed to him, "Kill high officials and distant yourself from your brothers and relatives", so Hu Hai had the sixth son of the First Emperor murdered in Duo (a place) and the twelfth son killed in Xianyang. Prince Jiang Lu and his two brothers were forced to commit suicide and before dying he cried tears and called out, "God, I'm not guilty". Prince Gao wished to flee, but was afraid his family would be killed, so he asked to be buried with his father, the First Emperor. "The Second Emperor was glad" and approved and gave money for the funeral. Hu Hai killed his brothers and his sisters. Historical books recorded 32 princes and princesses were killed.

Where were these princes and princesses buried? There was no record, but archaeological discoveries in the Qin Mausoleum area provide clues.

A group of attendant tombs was discovered in 1976 in Shang Jiao Village 350 metres east of the Outer City Wall of the Mausoleum. There are 17 tombs in a line running from south to north and the tombs are 2 to 15 metres apart. Among them 8 tombs have been excavated and each of them was in a shape of "甲" with a sloping passage into the burial chamber.

In the Qin Dynasty there was no entrance passage in the tombs of ordinary people, but only in the tombs of the royal family or high ministers. There wasn't a coffin in the tombs of ordinary people either, but coffins were excavated in these tombs. Both a well – made outer coffin, and an inner coffin, were excavated in six tombs, and an outer coffin was found in one tomb, but none in another. Seven human skeletons were found in the seven tombs and there were five males and two females. The age of the males was about 30 and that of the females around 20. There wasn't a skeleton, but a bronze sward in the eighth tomb. To the discovers' surprise, the skeletons in the coffins were scattered and some leg bones were in the earth outside the coffins. A skeleton was separated with legs and arms disconnected. A skull with an arrow head in its right side was even found outside a coffin. All the scattered skeletons implied that the inhabitants of the tombs died abnormally and some were killed by metal weapons and some killed by drawing (A cruel penalty——a criminal's arms and legs are tied with four horses and the horses draw to four directions).

Nevertheless, the burial objects in the tombs were valuable and they were gold, silver, copper, iron, jade, shells, and silk pieces. Among them a frog of silver was made vividly with fine techniques. It is 9. 5 cm. long and two Chinese characters "Prince House" were carved on an inner part of its mouth meaning it belonged in the Qin family. The tombs, coffins and rich burial objects indicate the grave occupants were high

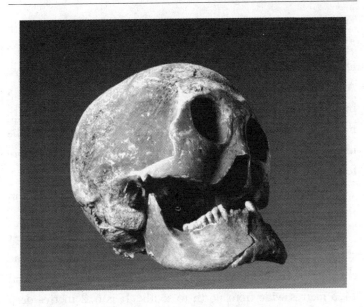

7 - 1   skull with an arrow

dignitaries, but the scattered remains told of their tragic fate. They were buried in the Qin Mausoleum and must have been relations of the First Emperor.

In these tomb ruins there was found burnt ash which the builders of the tombs burnt for warmth suggesting it was cold when these tombs were being built. The timing of the building of these tombs coincided with when the Second Emperor ordered the killing of the princes in the spring of 211 B. C. . So the remains may have been those of princes and princesses killed by the Second Emperor. Also two private seals made of copper were unearthed from the tombs. One with the Chinese words

"Rong Lu" was found in a man's tomb while another with "Ying Man" in a woman's tomb. There is a line between two characters and they are typical seals of the Qin Dynasty. Archaeologists deduced the one with "Rong Lu" might be a prince of the First Emperor and the other with "Yin Man" might be a princess of the First Emperor. We can expect the identities of the human remains will be established as more tombs are excavated.

Where is the tomb of Prince Gao who was mentioned in the "Historical Records"?

Archaeological workers found a tomb in the northwest corner of the Qin Mausoleum when exploring in 1978. The chamber of the tomb is 15 metre long from east to west and 14.5 metres wide from north to south. It is 6.2 metres deep below ground level and there is a 15.8 metre long sloping passage on its western side. It is the largest attendant Tomb of the Qin Mausoleum. It hasn't been excavated, but some ruins of ashes were found by drilling. Experts have deduced it was the tomb of Prince Gao who asked to be buried with the Qin First Emperor.

The "Historical Records" record that when the First Emperor was buried, all his concubines and maids who hadn't given birth were buried alive. All the workers who knew the secrets of the Mausoleum were sealed in the tomb because the Second Emperor was afraid they might reveal their secrets. It is not known how many concubines, maids and builders were buried alive with the First Emperor, but it is known to be the largest number of living burials in Chinese history. The burial place hasn't been found so far, but we are certain to find it in the future.

WHAT HAPPENED TO THE
QIN SECOND EMPEROR?

The Qin Second Emperor was a fatuous and incapable man who wallowed in sensual pleasures and drinking after he became Emperor. Zhao Gao had much power in the Court. He was a careerist and cruelly killed many generals and ministers as the opportunity arose. One day Zhao Gao pointed to a stag and deliberately told the Second Emperor it was a horse. In doing this he framed some loyal ministers. The cruel economic exploitation and political repression of the Second Emperor soon evoked strong opposition from the people. The Second Emperor began to complain to Zhao Gao and Zhao Gao, together with his son in law, planned the murder of the Second Emperor. Zhao's son in law led an army and broke into the Palace and demanded that the Second Emperor commit suicide. The Second Emperor begged to be given the title of a duke, or even be set free as a commoner, but was refused. The Second Emperor was eventually forced to kill himself. He was only 23 years old and had been in power for only three years.

The Second Emperor was buried as a commoner by Zhao

7-2   Picture of pointing to a stag and calling it a horse

Gao in Qujiang village (south of the Qujiang pool, Xi'an City, Shaanxi Province). The tomb is 4 metres high with a circumference of 10 metres and compared to the Qin Mausoleum, it is a tomb of a very ordinary person.

After the death of the Second Emperor, Zhao Gao allowed Zi Ying, one of the Second Emperor's nephews to become the Emperor of Qin. Zi Ying plotted against and killed Zhao Gao and the members of his family. However, Zi Ying was Emperor for only 46 days when the peasant insurrectionary army attacked the Capital. Zi Ying was forced to surrender, but was killed by General Xiang Yu, a leader of the peasant insurrectionary army. Xiang Yu not only killed Zi Ying but also other surviving princes and princesses. There isn't any historical record about where they were killed, or where they were buried, because nobody took any notice at the time.

7 - 3   Tomb of the Qin Second Emperor

VIII. ATTENDANT ANIMAL VAULTS DISCOVERED NEAR THE QIN TUMULUS

Besides the Terra-cotta Warriors and Horses located east of the Tumulus, 3 other kinds of life-sized pottery figures were discovered in the Qin Mausoleum Garden. These other pottery figures are: kneeling grooms, a large statue of the head groom and semi-naked pottery figures.

STABLE VAULTS IN THE QIN MAUSOLEUM GARDEN

A number of vaults with kneeling pottery figures and vaults containing real horse remains were discovered by exploratory drilling in late 1976 and early 1977. Some were scattered to the west of Shang Jiao village, east of the Tumulus and about 350 metres outside the outer city wall. Others were located between the inner and outer city wall, south-west of the mound. There are 93 vaults altogether and 37 of them have been excavated. There are 28 vaults of horses, 3 vaults of kneeling pottery figures and 6 vaults of pottery figures and horses together.

The vaults were in 3 rows running from north to south.

8 - 1   Kneeling pottery stockman

The horse vaults had a rectangular shape and one horse was in each vault with its head facing west. Some horses were lying on their side and some were in a crouching position. In some pits there were four holes in the floor and a partition wall with a board in the front part of the vault. The horse's legs were in the holes and the head was fixed in the board of the partition wall. These horses were buried alive. The horses lying on their side appear to have been buried alive also because the remains of bound horse feet could be seen. The horses in a crouching position seemed to have been killed and then buried.

There were clay lamps, clay vessels, clay basins, and iron sickles beside the heads of the horses. And in one vault there were a bronze plate, a bronze pot, 5 bronze rings beside the head of the horse. There were remains of millet and hay in some clay bowls and the bowls appear to have served as feeding bowls. The clay vessels were used for fetching water and the iron sickles were used to cut hay and grass for horses. The clay lamps indicated that the horses would be fed day and night.

The vaults of pottery figures were in a shape of a square and the figures were in boxes buried in the vaults. There were some clay vessels, clay lamps and iron sickles in front of the figures.

The vaults of the pottery figures and horses were of a rectangular shape and there was a stove in the western wall. Clay bowls, clay lamps and other burial objects lay beside the horses heads.

The skeletons of horses were excavated from the stable vaults and the horses were about 1.4 to 1.5 metres high and 1.5 to 1.6 metres long after assembling of the skeletons. They are the same size as the pottery horses unearthed from the vaults of the terra-cotta warriors and horses. Nine kneeling pottery figures wearing a long robe were unearthed. Each had a hair bun at the back of its head and a handsome face with a mustache. Some excavated burial objects had carved Chinese characters with meanings such as "middle stable", "palace stable", "left stable", "large stable, four dou". All these discoveries showed that the pits of stables were like the stables in the garden of Qin Shihuang's Palace and the kneeling pottery figures were grooms.

8 - 2　Big pottery figure of chief stockman

There was a large stable vault between the inner and outer

city wall, south of the Tumulus and it was in the shape of a carpenter's square. It was a hundred metres long and 9 metres wide. In the vault horse skeletons were crowded in rows. There were also two large pottery figures which were 1. 89 metres tall and of the same type as that in the vault of the Terra-cotta Warriors and Horses. The large figures wore a long robe with their hands inserted in each other's sleeves. Like the small vaults it also implied a stable in the Palace garden and the figures were grooms. The small horse vaults were severely damaged and there were probably 300 or 400 altogether. Together with the horses in the large vault of stable, about 500 or 600 horses were buried around the Qin Mausoleum.

The State of Qin was located in the west and was suited for raising horses. The Qin people were well – known for horse raising, and horses were the main means of transportation and a major force in warfare. There were stables in the garden of Qin Shihuang's Palace when he was alive. So the replica stables were built underground with many horses buried after the First Emperor's death. A large stable in the inner grounds and another in the outer grounds together with his terra-cotta army implied the First Emperor's determination to conquer the other six States.

VAULTS OF RARE BIRDS AND STRANGE ANIMALS

A group of attendant vaults was discovered between the

inner and the outer city wall in the south west part of the Qin Mausoleum Garden by an archaeological team between July 1977 and March 1978. There were 31 vaults in the group covering an area of about 2,000 square metres with a length of 80 metres from north to south and a width of 25 metres from east to west. The vaults were in three rows and the distances between the rows were 4.2 to 4.9 metres. There were 6 vaults in the first row, 17 in the second and 8 in the third row. Four vaults have been excavated and two are vaults of kneeling pottery figures and two are vaults with pottery coffins.

The size, and style of clothing, of the kneeling pottery figures were similar to the kneeling clay figures excavated from the stable vaults. They may have been handlers who tended the animals and fed the birds. The pottery coffins were about one metre long and 0.4 metres wide and there was a skeleton of an animal in each coffin. A zoologist determined that one might be an animal with teeth and a low crown, and the other might be grass – eating animal with teeth and a high crown. They might be strange animals which do not exist now. Some bird bones were discovered by exploratory drilling in the attendant vaults, but the bones were too small to identify what kinds of birds they were from. From the exploration the archaeologist determined that the first and the third row were vaults of kneeling pottery figures and the second row was vaults of rare birds and strange animals. "Han Jiu Yi", a historical book said, "In the Qin and Han dynasties there was an imperial garden covering 150 square kilometres in which there were lots of animals. Emperors went hunting there in autumn and winter." There were gardeners who managed the garden and handlers who tended the animals and fed the birds. Many attendant vaults in the Qin Mausoleum Garden were built as they were during the Qin Dynasty, so the vaults of rare birds and strange animals were located between the inner and outer city wall and were built for the same reasons.

VAULTS OF ANIMALS DISCOVERED
NORTH OF THE QIN TUMULUS

New attendant vaults were discovered in the north — eastern part of the Qin Mausoleum Garden by archaeological workers in early 1996. The construction of the vaults was of earth and wood structures similar to that of the vaults of Terra — cotta Warriors and Horses. There were two parts: a main vault and a sloping passage into the vault from the north. The vault was 23.5 metre long from north to south and 10 metres wide from east to west, and the sloping passage was 6 metres long and 4 metres wide. The total area covered was about 300 square metres. Nine partition walls divided the vault into 16 corridors. And each corridor was covered with wooden planks.

The vaults were damaged by fire and there were bird and animal bone remains in the vaults. After research the zoologist determined that there were dozens of birds and animals. The birds are thought to have been chickens, a large bird like a crane and others. The mammals could have been pigs, goats and dogs and the reptile is thought to have been a turtle. There were fish also. The dozens of birds and animals in these vaults have never been found before in the Qin Tomb. Many pottery fragments were also discovered in the vault indicating that there were pottery figures in the vault as well.

IX. WHO BUILT THE
QIN MAUSOLEUM?

The Qin Mausoleum was splendid, but its builders were even more impressive. Who designed the Qin Mausoleum? There is not any historical record. "HistoricalRecords" (written by Sima Qian in 100 B.C.) say the builders of the Qin mausoleum consisted of 700,000 captives, but is this correct? A few of the builders' graveyards were discovered in the Mausoleum Garden and some names of pottery workers were found on tiles and bricks excavated from the graves in recent years. Also some names of craftsmen were found on the terra－cotta figures and horses and on metal weapons.

WHO OVERSAW THE PROJECT OF
THE QIN MAUSOLEUM?

There is no historical record about who designed the Qin Mausoleum. The historical book "Han Jun Yi" says the Qin First Emperor instructed Li Si, his Prime Minister "to have 720,000 prisoners and captives build the Mausoleum according to the design." It shows that Li Si was the Project Manager of the Qin Mausoleum and there was a design drawing. Before Li

Si, four men, Lu Buwei, Chang Ping Jun, Wang Guan and Kui Lin had been Prime Ministers of Qin and they would have been in charge of the project then. However, both Lu Buwei and Li Si were the most important in the construction of the Mausoleum.

Lu Buwei was the first Prime Minister when the youthful Qin Shihuang became King of the State of Qin and he assumed much power. He was entitled "God Father" and was in charge of the Court. As Prime Minister he took an active role in the project of the Qin Mausoleum. Lu Buwei held the position of the Prime Minister for nine years and he established a good foundation for the building of the Mausoleum.

9−1   Graves of the builders of the Qin mausoleum

Li Si became Prime Minister after Kui Li and he also assumed an important role in building the Mausoleum because it was a large scale construction project. So the historical book recorded that Li Si oversaw the project. But of course, under him there were project teams which took charge of certain projects.

HOW MANY PEOPLE TOOK PART IN THE CONSTRUCTION OF THE PROJECT?

According to the "Historical Records", about 700,000 people took part in the building of the Qin Mausoleum. Construction of the Mausoleum commenced soon after Qin Shihuang was made prince to succeed the throne. The number of builders may have varied over the construction period. Many extra workers were summoned after he conquered the other six States and became the First Emperor. Some may have been taken to work on the Afang Palace, and then were called back to the site of the Mausoleum when the First Emperor died in 210 B.C.. After sealing of the Mausoleum some may have been sent back to the Afang Palace again. So the total number of the builders could have been 800,000 at times.

Innumerable builders died of hard work at the site because they did the hard physical work for years. Three graveyards of builders have been discovered to the west of the Qin Tumulus and the distances between them were about 500 metres. One was discovered in September 1978 and could be a hundred metres long, but it is severely damaged. Now only a small area of 0.5 metres long and 12 metres wide is preserved and there were many bones and human skeletons in it. The other graveyard was discovered by local farmers by accident in 1979 and excavated by archaeological workers later. It was 180 metres long from north to south and 45 metres wide from east to west with an area of about 8,100 square metres. 114 tombs were discovered and 103 of them were tombs of the Qin Dynasty and 11 were tombs of the Tang Dynasty (618 to 907 A.D.). 32 of the tombs of the Qin Dynasty were excavated and they were in a rectangular shape. The large ones were 10.6 metres long and 1.1 metres wide. The small ones were 1.1 metres long and 0.56 metres wide and they were the most of them. There were skeletons in the tombs and in some tombs there was one in each, but in some tombs there were two or three. There were even 14 skeletons in one tomb. 100 human skeletons were excavated from the 32 tombs and there were 3 female, 2 children of 6 to 12 years and 95 male of young and middle aged. 94 of the 100 skeletons were in a normal condition without signs of the reason of death. 6 of them were scattered about and the arm bones and legs were in piles and the body and skull were in separate parts. They might have been killed at the site. By accident, 18 plate tiles serving as epitaphs were discovered and from them it was possible to identify some as keepers and others as captives.

9-2   Pttery inscription"宫彊"(rubbing)

Names of craftsmen were found on the pottery vessels unearthed from the Qin Mausoleum Garden. They indicated that the craftsmen were from both the imperial pottery workshops and local workshops.

Carved and printed characters have been found on 500 terra-cotta warriors and horses excavated in the vaults so far. There were two kinds-numbers and characters. The numbers were for counting the number of warriors and horses they had made and the characters were the names of craftsmen who made the figures or horses. The numbers were carved by hand casually on the figures and horses when they were not dry. The numbers appeared on the horses' backs, necks, near their tails and on the warriors' backs, chests, necks or legs.

Most characters were roughly carved and fewer were printed in a formal way. They were visible on the warriors' legs, heads, chests and backs and on the horses' backs or necks. The characters could be divided into four kinds. The first was with the Chinese word "宫" (palace) and a single name of the craftsman. These were the sculptors from the imperial pottery workshops. Most characters with "宫水","宫彊","宫保" were inscribed at a secret spot under the robe of the warriors. The second kind was with names of places where the craftsmen came from and the names of the craftsmen such as "咸阳午" (Xianyang Wu). "咸阳" (Xianyang) was a name of a place and "午" (Wu) was the name of a craftsman. There were other names of places and names of craftsmen indicating the craftsmen came from Xianyang and other places. The third kind was with "右" (right) or "大" (great) and a single name of the craftsman. "右" (right) was a simple form for an official position and "大" (great) was a simple form for a master of craftsmen. So they were craftsmen who worked under the official, or master. The forth kind was with only names of craftsmen who made the figures or horses. They might be craftsmen from local workshops. The characters were very rough and simple and it could not be determined where the craftsmen came from.

By studying the characters we know that the sculptors and craftsmen who made the terra-cotta warriors and horses were from the imperial pottery workshops, from a pottery workshop in the capital city and from the local pottery workshops. The experts say that the warriors and horses made by sculptors from the imperial workshops were accurate and vividly coloured, while those made by craftsmen from the capital city and the local workshops were different. They were active and fresh with different styles. Some names of sculptors were seen on the figures and horses in Vault I, II and III, indicating that the figures and horses in all three vaults were made by the same sculptors and craftsmen at the same time.

The names of the makers could also be seen on weapons unearthed from the vaults of terra-cotta warriors and horses. They were on the side of halberds and the neck of spears.

THE BUILDERS OF THE QIN MAUSOLEUM

The Qin Mausoleum was built by working people with their blood and tears in the Qin Dynasty. An example is the transportation of stones. Thousands of people moved huge stones by hand, or with simple tools. There is still a huge stone a kilometre south-east of the Qin Tumulus which was left on the way because it was too heavy to be moved further.

The building of the Qin Mausoleum can be divided roughly into three phases. The first phase lasted 26 years from when Qin Shihuang succeeded to the throne to 221 B.C. when China was unified. While the Qin was fighting the other six strong states, many people may have been unable to take part in the construction. The second phase was about 9 years from Qin Shihuang's unification of China in 221 B.C. until his death. After Qin Shihuang defeated the other states and unified China, he concentrated a labour force and the finance and materials of the whole country on the construction of the Qin Mausoleum on a large scale. The third phase was the last of about 3 years from the death of the First Emperor to the Qin Second Emperor's third year.

The building of the Qin Mausoleum Garden lasted about 38 years but it was not finished. Some projects had to be stopped because of a peasant uprising in the Qin Second Emperor's third year and the builders were forced to fight the peasant army. However, these Qin forces were defeated. Some were killed in battle, but most were captured and buried alive by the peasant army.

According to the "Historical Records", the craftsmen and builders who knew the secrets of the Mausoleum were buried alive after the Qin First Emperor was buried, They were the most excellent craftsmen in the Qin Dynasty and their death caused the superb traditional technologies to be lost. The inscriptions on the pottery vessels and terra－cotta figures and horses excavated to date show the craftsmen came from 32 places across China. Some were from Shaanxi, Gansu, Henan, Hebei and Shaanxi provinces in North China and some from Jiangsu and Hubei provinces in South China. Others were from places which haven't been identified.

X. WAS THE
QIN MAUSOLEUM ROBBED?

The Mausoleum of the Qin First Emperor is famours for its magnificence and unprecedented rich burial objects. A consequence is that everyone who is interested in it is concerned if it has been robbed. Throughout the history of ancient China, all dynasties experienced confusion at their end providing opportunities for grave robbers. Most of the mausoleums of past dynasties were robbed during that time of confusion.

THE MAUSOLEUM WAS
DESTROYED BY XIANG YU

According to historical books, after entering the Qin Capital Xianyang, the peasant army general Xiang Yu killed Zi Yi, Third Emperor of Qin and his family members. He robbed the Palace and then set fire to the City of Xianyang burning it to ruins. After that, Xiang Yu led his army to the Qin Mausoleum Garden and ordered his soldiers to dig into the Tumulus. They took what they found and it was said that it took 300,000 people over 30 days to carry away the burial objects and other materials. The things which couldn't be carried away were burnt and the fire lasted many days. This might be the earliest and largest attempt to destroy to the Qin Mausoleum.

After Xiang Yu withdrew to the East, the Guangzhong plain where the Qin Capital was located was neglected and the Qin Mausoleum was left unguarded and uncared for. Grave robbers crowded into the Mausoleum and smashed up the outer coffin for copper. It was said that on one day goats of a shepherd boy ran into the grave left by the grave robbers. To find his goats the boy went into the grave holding a torch. Unfortunately a fire started and lasted for over 90 days. The fire damaged all the underground constructions and caused the ground architecture to collapse. Recent archaeological excavations showed that most of the attendant vaults and tombs were robbed and fired in the past.

THE QIN MAUSOLEUM AFTER THE QIN DYNASTY

After four years of war between their two peasant armies, Liu Bang defeated Xiang Yu and established the Western Han Dynasty. He adopted a series of policies to make the nation peaceful. In order to win popular support he ordered the protection of the Qin Mausoleum and arranged for 20 families to live in the Mausoleum Garden as keepers. Since then the Qin Mausoleum was protected by later dynasties. Song TaiZong of the Song Dynasty (960 to 1279 A. D.) ordered the executive officials of Lintong county to protect and repair the Qin Mausoleum in 970. Bi Yuan, Governor of Shaanxi set up a tablet for the Qin mausoleum in the Qing Dynasty (1636 to1911).

However, because of the buried riches in the Qin Mausoleum, it was inevitably coveted by some people throughout history. It was recorded that at the end of the Eastern Han Dynasty (25 to 220 A. D.), the Chimei insurrectionary army entered Chang'an, Capital of the Eastern Han and dug up the Qin Mausoleum. In the Wei Jin Period (220 to 420) the rulers of the late Zhao kingdom (319 to 350) were very greedy and dug up many tombs of past emperors and obtained a lot of treasure from them. They once dug up the Qin Mausoleum and took away copper pillars. Huang Chao, a leader of a peasant insurrectionary army led his troops into Chang'an, the then Capital and dug up the Qin Mausoleum in the late Tang Dynasty (618 to 907). In the early days of the Republic of China (1911 to 1949) warlords of Shaanxi also robbed the Mausoleum. Other nameless grave robbers were countless and the holes in the attendant tombs and vaults excavated now testify to it.

THE UNDERGROUND PALACE MAY NOT HAVE BEEN ROBBED

With the discovery and exhibition of the Terra-cotta

Warriors and Horses, as well as the bronze chariots and horses, more and more people have become interested in recent years in whether the Underground Palace of the Mausoleum was robbed. The Mausoleum is well protected now.

Some historical books record the Qin Mausoleum was robbed and burnt. If this was true the burial objects should have been destroyed first. But the two sets of unearthed bronze chariots and horses which used to lie in a chamber west of the Qin Tumulus beside the passage into the Underground Palace were not robbed or fired. This showed the Underground Palace might not have be robbed or burnt. During the last 10 years, archaeological workers have dug over 40,000 holes around the Qin Tumulus for exploratory research. This showed that there were four metre thick walls covered by bricks around the Palace. There were several passages into the Palace and no marks show they have been touched. Two holes one metre in diameter and 9 metres deep were found, but they were away from the Palace. That mercury existed under the Tumulus was proved coinciding with the descriptions in the "Historical Records". If the Underground Palace had been robbed the mercury would have flowed away. All these things show the Palace may not have been robbed.

From the unearthed cultural relics it has been found that the more valuable the burial objects are, the closer they were to the Underground Palace. The burial objects closest to the Tumulus must be more valuable than those in the attendant

UNITED NATIONS EDUCATIONAL,
SCIENTIFIC AND
CULTURAL ORGANIZATION

CONVENTION CONCERNING
THE PROTECTION OF THE WORLD
CULTURAL AND NATURAL
HERITAGE

*The World Heritage Committee
has inscribed*

The Mausoleum of the First Qin Emperor

on the World Heritage List

*Inscription on this List confirms the exceptional
and universal value of a cultural or
natural site which requires protection for the benefit
of all humanity*

DATE OF INSCRIPTION
-11 December 1987

DIRECTOR-GENERAL
OF UNESCO

10 − 1   Certificate given by the UNESO

vaults and tombs. We can be sure that when the Underground Palace is excavated, it will attract more visitors from home and abroad.

Some natural scientists, archaeologists and historians are now attempting to survey the secrets of the Underground Palace of the Qin Mausoleum using the latest scientific methods. The truth about whether the Palace was robbed and fired will be eventually known.

XI. THE BRONZE
CHARIOTS AND HORSES

The bronze chariots and horses excavated just west of the Qin Tumulus are treasures of world significance. When an archaeological team drilled an exploratory hole 20 metres west of the Qin Tumulus in July 1978, it discovered a round gold ornament from a depth of 7 metres, which was from a horse's head. After investigation, a large burial vault with 6 corridors and occupying a total area of 4,025 square metres was found. There were 6 rigs of painted wooden chariots and horses in the 3 southern corridors and 6 rigs of painted bronze chariots and horses in the northern ones.

With approval of the National Administration of Cultural Relics, the archaeological workers began to excavate the northern-most corridor in November 1980. The corridor was 11.8 metres long and 3.1 metres wide at the mouth, but 7 metres long and 2.1 metres wide at the bottom. There was a large wooden coffin in the corridor and two rigs of painted bronze chariots and horses were in it. The two rigs were designated No. 1 and No. 2. When excavated, the chariots and horses were severely damaged due to the decayed wooden coffin and the collapse of the earthen roofing. Fortunately their original locations were unaltered and pieces of the chariots and horses weren't missing.

The chariots and horses were moved to a restoration room of the Museum. After nearly 3 years of careful and painstaking restoration by archaeologists and other experts, No. 1 chariot and horses was put on public display opening to the public on October. 1, 1983. Four and a half years later, No. 2 chariot and horses opened to the public on May 1, 1988. Now they are on display in a special exhibition hall and are called the "Crown of the Bronze" and "Art Pearl".

11 – 1   Bronze chariots and horses

HISTORICAL KNOWLEDGE OF
CHARIOTS IN ANCIENT CHINA

Legend says chariots evolved from sledges. Later the middle part of the rounded wood was cut thinner to reduce the frictional drag of movement. A further reform was the separation of the wood. The middle part became an axle and the two sides became wheels. Traces of old chariots and carts have been discovered in some ancient civilized countries and China is a country which used chariots earliest in the world. According to a legend, the Xu tribe was famous for making chariots around 4,600 years ago. "Zuo Zhuan", a historical book, said the Xu tribe made chariots (21st to 17th century B. C.). Remains of a chariot made during the Shang period (16th to 11th century B. C.) were excavated in Anyang County, Henan Province and they showed an advanced technique of chariot making then.

Ancient chariots that have been found usually had a shaft and two wheels without spokes. Chariots and carts made around 2,200 B. C. had wheels with spokes. Spoked wheels were a significant improvement making the chariots or carts lighter and faster. Carts in Egypt had two wheels with 4 to 8 spokes per wheel, while carts in ancient China had two wheels with 18 to 30 spokes each.

The chariots and horses unearthed from the Qin

Mausoleum Garden were made of bronze and the decoration on them was of gold and silver. They are an exact half life-size model of the actual chariot, horse and driver. The bronze chariots, drawn by four horses with a single shaft, were placed one in front of the other. The front chariot, i.e. No. 1 chariot, was named "High Chariot" and the charioteer stood on the chariot. The rear chariot, No. 2, was named "Security Chariot". Its cabin was divided by a partition creating a front room and back room. In the front room sat the charioteer while the rear room was for the Emperor. The clothing and hair style of the two charioteers is similar to those of the generals unearthed in the vaults of the Terra-cotta Warriors and Horses.

THE FIRST EMPEROR'S TOURS OF INSPECTION

In ancient China each Emperor had his own special chariot and chariot team. The system of a chariot team started in the Shang Dynasty (16th to 11th century B. C.) and was completed in the Qin Dynasty. When the Qin First Emperor went on a tour of inspection, a very large chariot team followed. There were vanguard chariots, rear-guard chariots, company chariots of ministers and generals and company guard chariots in an order dictated by protocol. The unearthed bronze chariots imply the chariot system of the First Emperor.

After the Qin First Emperor unified China, he constructed straight roadways from the Capital, Xianyang, to major cities and cities on the frontiers. According to historical records the First Emperor went on large scale tours of inspection 5 times after 220 B. C.. He considered himself the First Emperor of China and wanted to show off. It is difficult to imagine how luxurious his chariot team was. It was said that a murderer wanting to kill the First Emperor, mistook a company chariot as the Emperor's because the company chariots were so luxurious.

Visitors to the bronze chariots and horses are surprised at the splendid and graceful shapes. The horses wear gold and silver halters. The chariots were painted in colour against a white background. On top of each chariot there is an oval – shaped umbrella – like canopy. No. 1 chariot seems to protect the following No. 2 chariot and the No. 2 chariot appears to be for the Emperor's spirit to go on tours of inspection.

The construction of the two chariots is almost identical, but their shapes are different.

No. 1 chariot and horses is 2.25 metres long and the total weight is 1,061 kilograms. The chariot has two wheels (diameter 66.4 centimetres), a single shaft and is drawn by four horses. The horses are almost the same, about 106 centimetres high, 109 centimetres long and each weights about 230 kilograms. The chariot body has an oblong shape and an umbrella stands in the middle. The canopy of the umbrella is a round bronze plate and the handle is shaped like bamboo. The charioteer stands under the umbrella, with a sword at his waist, holding 6 halters. There is a bronze bow in the front of the chariot and beside it is an arrow holder in which there are 54 arrows. On the other side there is a bronze shield which is the best preserved and earliest excavated.

11 – 2   Bronze shield on No 1 chariot and borses

The No. 2 chariot and horses is 3.17 metres long and the total weight is 1,241 kilograms. The chariot had two wheels (diameter 59 centimetres) and a single shaft which is longer than that of No. 1. The chariot is drawn by four horses which are the same as the horses of No. 1 chariot. It has two rooms, the front one for the charioteer and the rear one perhaps for the spirit of the Emperor. The charioteer is kneeling in the front room with a sword at his waist, holding halters. The rear room has a door at the back and has a window in each of its two sides and in the front partition. The windows can be easily opened and closed and there are small holes in the windows for ventilation. When the windows are open, the inside of the chariot is cool. When they are closed, the inside is warm. So the chariot is also called the "air – conditioned chariot".

THE CHARIOTS AND HORSES SHOW THE ADVANCED DESIGN AND MANUFACTURING ABILITIES OF THE QIN DYNASTY

Prior to the excavation of the bronze chariots and horses, many remains of ancient chariots and horses had been discovered. However, archaeologists were unable to find the means by which the chariot was drawn by the horses until they studied these bronze chariots and horses. This was because wooden chariots rotted and earlier unearthed bronze chariots were too small or rough to show clearly.

The chariots had a single shaft with its rear end connected to the axle. Both the shaft and axle supported the body of the chariot and between them was padding to reduce bumping. There was a yoke on either side of the shaft and two horses were harnessed in each yoke. The outside horse on either side wore tassels and the four horses were linked with reins and pulled the chariot together. This method of harnessing assists the horses to run quickly and also conserve effort.

The chariot is composed of 3,462 pieces, of which 1,742 are made from bronze, 737 from gold and 983 are made of silver. Everyone who sees them can appreciate the advanced technology and admire the artistic shapes. For instance, the roof umbrella is only four millimetres thick while the window is one millimetre thick, with many ventilation holes. The horse tassels were made of bronze thread as thin as a hair. The horse necklets were welded together with 42 nodes of gold and 42 nodes of silver. Archaeologists can examine the welded joints only with the help of magnification. According to research, the making of the bronze chariot and horses involved different techniques such as casting, welding, riveting, mounting, embedding and carving. The chariots and horses showed the advanced design and construction of chariots and metallurgical techniques of the Qin Dynasty.

XII. NEW DISCOVERIES IN THE QIN MAUSOLEUM GARDEN

In September, 1999, the Shaanxi Provincial Government held a Press Conference in the City of Xi'an and Vice Governor Zhao Dequan announced new discoveries in the Qin Mausoleum Garden to TV News Reporters and journalists from China and overseas. He reported that the Shaanxi Government had decided to establish an Armour Museum of the Qin Dynasty on a new historical site. With the Museum of Qin Shihuang's Terra-cotta Warriors and Horses and the Museum of Chariots and Horses it will form a group of museums on their historical sites which is the largest in China and even the world.

UNEARTHED STONE ARMOUR CORRECTED A LONG—HELD BELIEF AMONGST HISTORIANS

Chinese historians used to believe that helmets weren't worn in the Qin Dynasty, but the discovery of a vault containing stone armour corrected this long—held belief.

Farmers from Xiachen Village, southeast of the Qin Mausoleum were doing farm work when they found fired red soil in September, 1996. They reported it to the archaeologists who paid considerable attention because, from their experience, fired red soil usually implied a site of a ground construction or an underground construction. After exploratory drilling it was apparent it was an attendant vault. Researching the site in April and May, 1997 they ascertained the shape and construction of the vault. From July 1998 to January 1999 the archaeologists again explored the vault and attempted to excavate sections.

The vault, located about 200 metres southeast of the Tumulus, has an oblong shape being 130 metres long from east to west and 100 metres wide from north to south, covering an area of 13,689 square metres. It is as large as Vault I of the Terra-cotta Warrior and Horses and is the largest attendant vault discovered so far between the inner and outer city walls. At the time of writing, 145 square metres of the vault have been excavated.

The method of construction of the vault is almost the same as the Vaults of the Terra-cotta Warriors and Horses. The top of vault is 0.3 to 4 metres below ground level and the vault is 3.5 to 4 metres deep. There is a sloping entry ramp at each corner and the vault was divided into several parts by rammed earth partition walls. Like Vault I of the Entombed Army it is an earth － and － wood structure in the shape of a covered corridor. Within the chamber, there are earth － rammed and wood － covered partition walls, across which huge and strong rafters were placed, then covered with mats and fine soil and filling earth. The floors were paved with wood also. Fired red soil was found when the vault was first excavated. Archaeologists then found a layer of ash 10 to 20 centimetres thick. They concluded that the vault had been set on fire as were the vaults of the Terra-cotta Warriors and Horses. In the corridor 87 suits of blue - gray stone armour and 43 stone helmets have been unearthed from an excavation covering an area of 75 square metres. Besides these, some bronze arrowheads, broken Terra-cotta figures and pieces of bronze chariots and horses were also unearthed.

The unearthed stone armour can be divided into three kinds: large, medium and small sized. Each suit of armour comprises more than 700 thin, overlapping stone tiles sewn together with copper thread. Each suit measures 80 centimetres long and weighs about 20 kilograms. The suits of armour are similar to those worn by the Terra - cotta warriors. The overlapping stones were well made and have various shapes according to their use in the different parts of the suit. Large overlapping stones are 7 to 8 centimetres long and 3 to 4 centimetres wide and the small ones are 3 to 4 centimetres long and 1 centimetre wide, with both being 0.2 to 0.3 centimetres thick. At each end of the overlapping stone there are 4 to 8 small holes for sewing.

The helmets are crowned with a circular stone from which jade and pearl ornaments hung. Overlapping stone shingles hang from small holes that line the circular stone's perimeter. The stone shingles hang 30 centimeters from the top of the helmet to the wearer's shoulders.

The difference between the stone armour and the armour on the Terra-cotta warriors is the helmet. When the Terra-cotta warriors were excavated, archaeologists didn't find any helmets in the pits. Therefore some archaeologists concluded that helmets weren't worn in the Qin Dynasty. The discovery of the stone helmets altered this belief.

The suits of stone armour were placed in a regular order with four suits in each line forming four columns in each corridor similar to how the Terra-cotta warriors stand in Vault I. It is thought that the armours originally were hung on wooden frames, but dropped to the ground after the wooden frames were burnt. A very large suit of stone armour, with overlapping stones 15 centimetres in length, was also found. It is about 1. 8 metres long after restoration. Archaeologists believe the suit wasn't for a soldier, but for a horse.

The stone armour couldn't be worn in battle because it was too heavy. The vault of armour, like the vaults of the Entombed Army, was constructed because the First Emperor wanted everything after death to be like when he was alive. So some archaeologists think the vault was a store of weapons. Besides the stone armour there could be wooden chariots and Terra-cotta figures and horses in the vault. However, this will be established only after further excavation.

THE FIRST "DING" IN THE QIN MAUSOLEUM
HAS BEEN UNEARTHED

The discovery of the stone armour vault provided an important clue for archaeologists to find other new attendant vaults. The archaeologists carried out systematic exploration around the vault of armours and in March 1999 found a new attendant vault 40 metres to the south. The vault is in "凸" shape and is 70 metres long from east to west and 12.5 to 16 metres wide from north to south, covering an area of 800 square metres. The structure is almost identical to the vault of armours.

A large bronze "ding" (Chinese name for a cauldron - shaped vessel on three squat legs) was unearthed from the vault standing 0.6 metres tall and weighing 212 kilograms. It is the largest Qin ding ever found. The diameter of the ding is 60.5 centimetres and the ding is elaborately shaped with magnificent decorative patterns. The legs of the ding feature animal face patterns. From the decoration and type the ding is thought to have been made in the middle of the Warring States period (475 to 221 B. C.), or earlier, and to have served as a sacrificial vessel in a temple where the ancestors of the Qin First Emperor were worshipped. Experts surmise that the ding may have been moved from the temple to hide it during the turmoil at the end of the Qin Dynasty. The ding is a valuable relic for the study of the ritual system and technique of bronze casting in the Qin Dynasty.

POTTERY FIGURES DEPICTING
AN ACROBATIC TROUPE OF ACROBATIC
PERFORMERS HAS BEEN UNEARTHED

In the chamber of the pit, archaeologists were surprised to find 11 life－sized pottery figures with distinctive characteristics scattered within an excavated area of 9 square metres. Like those in the vaults of Terra-cotta Warriors and Horses, the pottery figures were broken into pieces, but each could be identified basically. The figures wore skirts just long enough to cover their hips. Diamond and star－shape patterns were painted on their skirts.

These figures are of different sizes and feature graceful poses. Three of them have been restored except for their severely damaged heads and were named No. 1, 3 and 5 according to the order of discovery. The No. 1 figure, comparatively small in size, stands straight with his hands clasped in front of his belly. No. 3 figure is the winner of a competition raising his right hand in the air with his waist swaying and his belly bulging. The No. 5 figure, about two metres tall after full restoration, stands upright grasping a horizontal tube－shaped bar with both hands, and holds a long vertical pole with his right arm. Originally all the figures were colourfully painted, but unfortunately the colour has faded due to time or fire. The Chinese characters "咸阳亲" (Xianyang Qin) and "高" (Gao) were found inside figures No. 1 and 5 and these are thought to be the names of the craftsmen and the name of places from where they came.

Experts believe that the pottery figures unearthed from the vault depict acrobatic performers buried to serve the First Emperor underground in his afterlife.

There are no historical records of these vaults and they had not been found during former exploratory drilling. They are located between the inner and outer city walls and their burial order of importance would be higher than the vaults of the Terra-cotta Warriors and Horses. The discovery of the two vaults are very important and will greatly assist archaeologists study the Qin Mausoleum, the Qin Dynasty and the layout of the mausoleum in the ancient China.

XIII. NEW THOUGHTS ABOUT THE DISCOVERY OF THE ENTOMBED TERRA – COTTA ARMY

The existence of Qin Shihuang's Terra-cotta warriors and horses were not recorded in Chinese history books or documents. They disappeared from view when the Qin Dynasty was overthrown, and were discovered only by accident.

13 – 1   Former view of the ground where the Terra – cotta Warriors and Horses excavated before

THE DISCOVERY OF A "POTTERY GOD" WITH THE DIGGING OF A WELL

When you visit Vault I of the Qin Terra-cotta Warriors and Horses, you will be struck by the magnificent terra-cotta army. However, if you look carefully you will find a sign in the south – east corner which says "This was where the discovery well was dug". The well's location was 1,500 metres east of Qin Shihuang's Tumulus and it used to be covered with brambles.

13 – 2   Location of the well dug by local peasants who found the Entombed Army

On March 29, 1974, local farmers from Xiyang, a small village 7.5 km. east of Lingtong County were digging a well

south of their village when they found a hole. They dug further
into the hole and found pottery fragments, bronze arrowheads
and crossbows. The astonished farmers guessed there must be
pottery statue of a god in the hole. In the evening old men
came to the site to burn joss sticks and pray to the god to not be
blamed.

NEWS REACHES THE GOVERNMENT LEADERSHIP

When the local farmers didn't know what to do with the
"pottery God", Fang Shumin (from Yanzhai Township), a
cadre responsible for irrigation work, came to inspect the well.
He knew a little about archaeology and when he saw the pottery
and brick fragments he was sure they were cultural relics. He
asked the farmers to stop digging and reported to the
Government of Lintong County. Zhao Kangmin and other two
workers responsible for archaeological affairs from the Lingtong
Culture Club were sent to investigate. The three were stunned
by what they saw. They had never seen fragments from what
were obviously large pottery figures. Unable to date them,
they decided to take the fragments back to the Culture Club.
They told the farmers about the National Policy on Archaeology
and asked them to hand over all the things found. During the
following two months Zhao Kangmin and his workers restored
three figures. Because they were unsure of their historical
period, they did not report the discovery to the relevant

department.

13 – 3   The earliest found terra – cotta figures shown in the
Museum of Lintong County

By coincidence, Lin Anwen, a journalist from the Beijing – based China News Agency, was in Lingtong to visit his family. He chanced to see the three restored figures because his wife worked in the Culture Club. From experience he knew they were models of Qin Shihuang soldiers over 2000 years old and rare treasures. After having interviewed Zhao Kangmin and made further investigations, he wrote an article entitled "Terra – cotta Warriors and Horses of the Qin Dynasty Unearthed in the Tomb Area of the First Emperor". He sent the article to the Editor of "The People's Daily" where it was published in the "Situation Collection" which was read by Chinese high officials and it caught the attention of the Central

Government. On June 30, Li Xiannian, then China's Vice – premier, instructed "I suggest that the State Cultural Relics Administration discuss with the Shaanxi Provincial Government what immediate action to take to properly protect this key relic site." Hence the Terra – cotta figures became known to, and cherished by, the world.

THE TERRA – COTTA FIGURES HAD BEEN FOUND BEFORE

The pits of Terra – cotta warriors and horses were only about 5 metres below ground level, but they were not recorded in Chinese history. They had been found before, but were not known to the public before they were discovered in 1974.

When visiting the Terra – cotta figures you will see pottery fragments under the fallen logs and cross – beams in the vaults and traces of burnt charcoal and ash on the partition walls. The latter show the vaults had been damaged. According to records and analysis of the archaeological excavation, it might have been Xiang Yu, one of the two generals who overthrew the Qin Dynasty, who destroyed the Terra – cotta figures along with other constructions within the tomb area at the end of the Qin Dynasty. He may have ordered his soldiers to dig up the pits, damage the pottery figures and set fire to them. So the soldiers might have been the earliest people who found, then destroyed the Terra – cotta statues.

13 - 4   Terra - cotta warrior and horses being excavated

From the excavations, it became established that the ground of the vaults became wasteland in the late Western Han Dynasty (206 B. C. to 24 A. D.). In one of the partition walls in Vault I a tomb of the early Western Han was found and a coin made in the time of the Han Emperor Wu was discovered in the tomb. Several tombs were found in Vault I and a joint husband and wife tomb of the Ming Dynasty (1368 to 1644) was even lain beneath the brick floor of the terra - cotta figures. Two tombs of the Han Dynasty and 12 tombs of modern times were also found in Vault II. A 10 metres deep well, dug in the late Ming Dynasty or early Qing Dynasty (1644 to 1911), was found in Vault II and there were many pottery fragments in it. From this, it can be seen the terra – cotta figures were disturbed when these tombs were built and the well dug.

The local farmers reported their ancestors had seen pottery fragments when they built tombs or dug wells there, but thought them to be from "strange figures". In August 1974, when experimental drilling was being done in Vault I, He Wanchun, a 69 year old local farmer told the archaeological experts a story. When 13 years old (around 1918), his father had dug a well. While digging he found a life – sized "strange figure" and he damaged one of its arms. The well initially had water, but became dry after two years. The farmers thought the "strange figure" might have drunk all the water so they removed it from the well and smashed it to pieces. He Wanchun showed the experts where his father had dug the well and it was within Vault I.

The terra – cotta figures had been found in history, but they were not considered to be treasures. Thanks to the local archaeological workers and the journalist from the News Agency, they were protected and made public. Then with the help of governments at each level, archeological experts have been excavating and studying them and have been able to tell the real story of the terra – cotta warriors and horses.

XIV. THE OUTSTANDING ARCHAEOLOGICAL PROJECT OF THE CENTURY

As a treasure of historical culture the Qin First Emperor's terra – cotta army was produced in ancient China, re – discovered at the end of the 20th century and will be protected forever.

The discovery of the terra – cotta figures attracted attention from all levels of the Chinese Government. An excavation team was organized in 1974 and excavation at the Mausoleum got under way and has proceeded since according to plan. On July 15, 1975, the Chinese News Agency published the news "A large vault was discovered east of the Qin First Emperor's burial mound and many previously unseen terra – cotta warriors and horses have been unearthed". It was the first time the news was published to the world, which had a great impact within China and in the world at large. A Museum was established on the excavation site by the National Government.

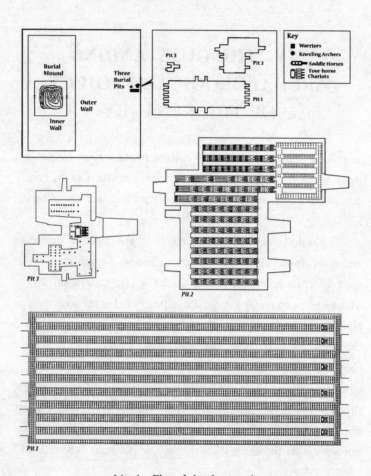

14-1 Plan of the three vaults

VAULT I WAS THE FIRST
EXCAVATED AND EXHIBITED

Establishment of the Museum commenced in 1976 before the vault was re – filled with earth to protect the terra – cotta figures and horses. While preparing for construction archaeologists did exploratory drilling around the Mausoleum. They found the second vault north east of Vault I on April 23, 1976 naming it Vault II. Then the third vault was found northwest of Vault I on May 11.

An incomplete pit was also found between Vault II and III, but there weren't any terra – cotta statues in it. The incomplete pit was dug at the same time as the other three, but was stopped because of the peasant uprising at the end of the Qin Dynasty.

It is estimated that about 8,000 life – sized terra – cotta figures and horses, a hundred chariots and over 100,000 bronze weapons will be unearthed from the three vaults.

As soon as the main structure of the Exhibition Hall over Vault I was finished in April 1978, excavation re – commenced. The vault was divided into 27 excavation areas and one – third of it have been excavated to date, covering an area of 2,000 square metres. 1,087 terra – cotta warriors and horses (taking in one – sixths of the estimated total), 8 ruins of chariots, 32 terra – cotta horses and a lot of bronze weapons have been unearthed. The Museum and Vault I opened to the public on October 1, 1979.

The excavation in Vault I is proceeding according to plan. The vault is in an oblong shape, 230 metres long from east to west, 62 metres wide from north to south and 5 metres deep, covering an area of 14,260 square metres. The western end of the vault is 1,225 metres away from the eastern side of the outer city wall. There are 10 earth – rammed partition walls dividing the vault into 9 corridors and a corridor running around the circumference of the vault. There are 5 sloping entry ramps into each of the eastern and western sides of the vault.

In the long corridor at the eastern end of the vault stand 210 terra – cotta warriors in three rows. 204 face east and 3 at the northern and southern end face north and south respectively. Two warriors with high – tied hair in the middle row at the northern and southern ends appear to be generals of the vanguard. The weapons unearthed with the warriors were crossbows, bronze bows, bronze arrow – heads, bronze swords, halberds and spears. From hand gestures of the 175 restored warriors, 164 of them held crossbows and another 11 held spears and halberds. Some of them had bronze swords at their waists. So the three rows are regarded as the vanguard armed mainly with crossbows.

In the long corridor at the western end of the vault also stand three rows of terra – cotta warriors. The outer western row faces west while the inner two rows face east. Because they haven't been excavated, the numbers of warriors and weapons aren't known, but it is expected that the number is the same as in the eastern corridor. They are thought to be the rear guard.

In the right and left corridors there are two rows of terra – cotta warriors each with the outside row facing outwards. Each row is about 184 metres long and around 180 terra – cotta warriors may be unearthed. Except for figures at the eastern ends wearing robes, most are armoured warriors with crossbows as their main weapons, but some had swords at their waists.

In addition to the corridor around the circumference, there are 9 corridors in the vault and in each corridor there are four columns consisting of chariots and charioteers and infantrymen facing east. Thus there are 36 columns in the 9 corridors and each column is 178 metres long. From the excavation in Vault I, the formation of the chariots and infantrymen is known to be as follows: there are three warriors on each chariot and infantrymen around it. Three rows, with 4 infantrymen in each row, stand in front of the chariot as a vanguard. The numbers of infantrymen behind each chariot is different with 70 behind some and 100 behind others. This formation with a chariot as the centre and infantrymen around strengthened the infantrymen shielding the chariot.

For the following reasons it is thought that the troops in Vault I are in a defensive formation, not marching or in an attacking formation:

1) the crossbows which the warriors had as their main weapon were used for long distant archery, not short range attack;

2) there is a row around the circumference facing outwards so the army does not have a concentrated attacking direction;

3) most of the vanguard in the eastern end are in robes and not armoured. It is a well – organized, united, but flexible army formation with a vanguard, rear guard and flanks.

VAULT II WAS EXHIBITED
WHILE BEING EXCAVATED

When exploratory drilling was done around Vault I, the second pit was discovered north of the eastern end of Vault I on April 23, 1976. It was called Vault II. From May 1976 to August 1977 an archaeological team did a proving excavation on Vault II and determined that the vault, in a "L" shape, covered an area of 6,000 square metres, half the size of Vault I. It consists of two parts, or four arrays, and the northern part is in an oblong shape and the southern part in a square shape. In the proving excavation there was unearthed 11 wooden chariots, 67 pottery chariot horses, 32 terra – cotta cavalrymen, 29 pottery horses, 163 terra – cotta warriors and about 900 bronze weapons of various types.

To protect Vault II, the Provincial Government decided to build a protective exhibition hall over the site. The hall, covering an area of 12, 000 square metres and having a construction area of 17, 016 square metres, commenced construction in September 1988. It uses natural light and is fitted with equipment to keep the hall at a constant temperature. The hall is in the shape designed to combine the tradition of ancient architecture and modern teaching. The formal excavation in Vault II started on 1 March, 1994 and from the proving excavation it is estimated that 89 wooden chariots, 261 charioteers, 365 chariot horses, 116 cavalrymen, 116 horses, 562 infantrymen and a lot of bronze weapons will be unearthed.

Vault II opened to the public on 14 October, 1994 and it is being exhibited while excavation, restoration and research is going on. To date, dozens of cavalrymen, infantrymen and horses from the first array and the fourth array have been unearthed. Others were excavated on the surface of rafter ruins. According to the plan, one − third of the pit will not be excavated and the rafter ruins will be left undisturbed, one − third will be excavated and the broken terra − cotta figures and horses will be left as discovered and the remaining one − third will be excavated and the broken terra − cotta figures and horses restored.

Vault II is divided into four arrays according to the shape of the vault and the different military forces. The first array, i. e. , the eastern protruding part of the vault is 26. 6 metres long and 38. 8 metres wide. There are 174 standing archers along the outside on the four sides and 160 kneeling archers in 8 columns in the middle. The formation of standing and kneeling archers allows the archers to shoot in turns. The second array, located in the south of the vault, is 52 metres long and 48 metres wide including 8 passage ways. It is comprised of 64 chariots, 8 in each of the passage ways. Each chariot carries three warriors with the middle one the charioteer. The third array in an oblong shape located in the middle of the vault, 68 metres long and 16 metres wide. It is a formation of chariots, infantrymen and cavalrymen. There are 8 columns and in each column there are 6 chariots. Behind the chariots there are infantrymen and a few cavalrymen. The fourth array, located in the north of the vault, is 50 metres long and 20 metre wide. It is composed of 6 chariots and 124 saddled horses and cavalrymen. The four arrays form a single formation, but they can also act independently as separate arrays.

The excavation in Vault II is a large project and can be roughly divided into 3 stages:

1) removal of the earth from the rafter ruins,

2) excavation of the archers in the first array and cavalrymen in the fourth array,

3) excavation of chariots, infantrymen and cavalrymen in the second and third arrays.

VAULT III APPEARS TO BE THE HEADQUARTERS

Vault III was discovered to the northwest of the Vault I and to the west of Vault II with exploratory drilling on May 11, 1976. Excavation started in 1989 and Vault III was found to be very different from Vaults I and II. It was opened to public in September 1989.

Vault III is in a "U" shape with a total area of 500 square metres. There is a sloping entry ramp on its eastern side opposite which is a chariot and horse house. On both sides of the house there is a winging room. From this vault there were unearthed one wooden chariot, 68 terra – cotta warriors, four terra – cotta horses and 34 bronze weapons. The unearthed figures and horses were severely damaged and most of the heads and some other parts haven't been found. It is a mystery as to who damaged them and when.

The arrangement of the pottery figures is quite different from Vaults I and II in which the warriors are in battle formation. Those in Vault III are arrayed opposite each other along the walls in rows. The number of figures is much less than in Vaults I and II, and they seem to be guards of honour. The hair tie styles and weapons of the 68 warriors are also different from those in other two vaults with the latter armed with long – range crossbows and arrows and short range weapons such as spears, barbed spears and swords. In Vault

III only one kind of weapon was found, called "shu", which had no blade and is believed to be used by guards of honour.

The chariot in Vault III is different from that in Vaults I and II. The former was decorated with bright colours and had a painted 42 centimetre diameter canopy. There are no weapons, but 4 warriors in the chariot. From the dress and hand gestures of the warriors it seems that their position is higher than the charioteers, but lower than the officers in the other two vaults. So the chariot is believed to be a command chariot.

The remains of deer — horn and animal bone were also discovered in the northern winging room, which was never found in Vaults I and II. The archaeologists think it is probably the place where sacrificial offerings and the saying of prayers were practiced.

The location of Vault III at the left end of Vault I and the rear of Vault II implied its importance. The figures and horses unearthed from Vault III are basically the same as those in other two pits showing they were made at the same time and all were built as a complete unit. Judging from all the above, Vault III is most likely the headquarters directing the underground army. It is a vivid record of the earliest headquarters discovered so far in China and it provides an invaluable object for military scientists to research the army system of the Qin Dynasty.

XV. STRUCTURE OF THE VAULTS AND THE METHODS OF MAKING THE TERRA-COTTA WARRIORS AND HORSES

Although the vaults of the terra-cotta warriors and horses were created over 2,200 years ago, then damaged by fire, the magnificent appearance of their large structure can still be seen. More secrets will be discovered by archaeological excavation and study of the structure of the vaults, the types of terra-cotta warriors, the battle formation of the terra-cotta army and the methods of making the terra-cotta figures and horses. The vaults provide extremely valuable material and data for research of the Qin Dynasty.

ARCHITECTURAL STRUCTURE OF THE VAULTS

Visitors are often surprised to see the large scale and magnificent battle formation of the terra-cotta army of the First Emperor. The Qin army was famous for its great size, even as early as in Qin Duke Mu's period (Warring States 475 to 221 B. C.). The vaults of the terra-cotta warriors and horses were constructed after the Qin unification of China. The Qin First Emperor collected taxes, materials and skilled craftsmen from across the whole country for the construction of his Mausoleum. These three attendant vaults, covering a total area of 40,000 square metres, had their special architectural forms and characteristics. They were a total battle array, but could also be divided into independent army units.

Vault I, in a rectangular shape, is 230 metres long, 62 metres wide, covering an area of 14,260 square metres. It is 1,225 metres away from the Qin tumulus, in a straight line from the northeastern corner of the outer City Wall of the Qin Mausoleum. In the vault there are 10 two metre high earth – rammed walls which divided the vault into 9 corridors from north to south and an outside circumferential corridor. There are 5 sloping entry ramps in each four sides of the vault.

The shape of the Vault II is different from that of the Vault I. It is in shape of a carpenter's square, covering about 6,000 square metres. There are two vaults: the northern part is a square – shaped and the southern part is an oblong – shaped. Both are earth – wood structure in a form of roofed corridors. The longest part from east to west is 120 metres and the widest part from north to south is 98 metres. There are two sloping entrances in the eastern, western and northern ends respectively.

Vault III, called "the headquarters pit" is in shape of a "U", covering an area of 520 square metres. In its eastern end there is a sloping entry ramp, 11.2 metres long, 3.7 metres wide, opposite which is a chariot and horse house. On both sides of the house there is a chamber.

As the underground structures are on a large scale and with special forms, careful plans should be done in each process according to the design. The plans of the three vaults are different, but the three dimensional method of construction is the same. They are all earth − wood structures in the form of roofed corridors. The process of construction is as follows:

Long vaults were dug first, and then soil was piled up and rammed to set up a base and the partition wall. When the partition walls were built, wood was placed against the walls. Across this standing wood, rafters were placed and then covered with mat, a 10 to 30 centimetres thick layer of fine soil and finally a 2 metre thick covering of earth. The floor was paved with brick. After the tunnels had been built, the chariots and terra − cotta warriors and horses were carried into them through the sloping entrances and arranged in order. After completing the arrangement, the entrances were shut off with wood lining and the sloping ramps were filled with rammed earth. It finally formed a completely sealed underground structure.

HOW MANY TYPES OF WARRIORS AND HORSES ARE THERE?

The terra − cotta warriors unearthed from the three vaults can be divided into three types: infantry, charioteers and

15 - 1   A terra - cotta senior army officer

passengers, and cavalry. The infantry, including figures in lines of battle formation and figures in front and behind the chariots, can be subdivided into generals, officers and warriors. The generals and officers are of two types: those wearing robes (light armoured figures) and others wearing armour (heavy armoured figures). The warriors can also be subdivided into figures holding cross bows, those holding short - handled

15 - 2   A terra - cotta warrior with armour

weapons and others holding long - handled weapons. The figures holding cross bows are standing archers and kneeling archers. The figures holding short - handled weapons have swords or hooks. The figures holding long - handled weapons have spears, halberds, lances, "shu" (a weapon without a blade used by guards of honour) or others weapons. On each ordinary chariot, there were two soldiers, and a charioteer. On the commander's chariot there is a general, a charioteer and one or two soldiers. The cavalry is divided into those in the battle formation and those in the rear.

The pottery horses are of two types: those drawing chariots and those for riding.

A NEW UNDERSTANDING OF QIN UNIFORMS PROVIDED BY THE TERRA−COTTA FIGURES

The discovery of the terra−cotta warriors and horses helps us know more about the uniforms of the soldiers in the Qin Dynasty. The soldier wore a hat, robe, trousers, belt and shoes.

The hats worn by warriors were a crown−hat, or a cap. The crown−hat, which was a symbol of rank, was usually worn by generals. The crown−hat with a single sloping flat plate was for lower officers. The crown−hat with double flat plates was for middle level officers and generals. The crown−hat with special double ties was for high generals. Caps were of two different types, one for armoured warriors and the other for the cavalry.

Most terra−cotta warriors wore long robes long enough to cover the knee. The robes were of two types: double layered robes for high generals and single layer robes for other generals and warriors. A short−sleeved robe was found which was for the cavalry. This was adapted from robes worn by people of the Hu nation who were good at horse riding. It was also found that soldiers wore a round collared shirt under their robes.

15 - 3   A terra - cotta archer in the pose of
shooting a bow and arrow

Trousers worn by warriors had both long and short legs.
The long legged trousers reached the ankles and were tied at the
ankle. These were worn mainly by generals, officers and the
cavalry. The short legged trousers didn't cover the knees.
Most of the armoured warriors and charioteers had long cords
wound around their calves which seemed to be for the
protection of their calves.

Warriors wore shoes made of gunny cloth. The shape of the shoe was like a ship with a lower front and a high rear. It had a thin sole. The remaining colour shows that the shoes were painted black or brown but the edges were red. The cavalry wore 15 centimetres high boots. From the remaining colour it is thought the boots were painted red, or green.

The clothes and shoes worn by warriors show a combination of the customs of the Han people and the Hu people (a minority nationality in China). The main colours of the clothes were green, red, blue and purple with strong contrasts. The study of the various colours and styles of the clothing show that the uniforms were not made by the state, but by the soldiers themselves.

HOW WERE THE FIGURES AND HORSES MADE?

The terra-cotta figures and horses were all broken when unearthed. From the broken pieces it can be analyzed that there were 4 steps in manufacture: molding and sculpting, carving, firing and painting.

The bodies of the terra-cotta warriors were made in molds, or by sculpting. The feet, hands and legs were made by hand and then joined to the body. The most sophisticated technique was manufacture of the head. Two molds were used to make the face and other parts of the head and then the two halves were joined together. Ears, nose, hair and moustache were made separately and added later. In order to stop the figures toppling over, a plinth was added beneath the feet of the warrior. The roughly made models were carved exquisitely in detail according to their personal characters and rank. After the figures had been made they were carried into kilns and fired. In order to prevent the figures from deforming or exploding, one, two or three small holes were made in the body

15 - 4   A terra - cotta battle - robed warrior

before firing. The last step of manufacture was painting with colour.

The technique of making the terra – cotta horses was similar to that of the terra – cotta warriors. The head, body, legs, and tail of the horse were made in molds separately. The ears were made by hand. They were then all joined together and the joins covered with clay. Like the terra – cotta warriors, they were carved, fired and painted with colour.

A PEARL OF THE ANCIENT ORIENTAL ARTS

The discovery of the terra – cotta warriors and horses was one of the great events in the history of the arts of China and the world as well. The terra – cotta warriors, with characteristics of realism, a style of simple, but fine technique and a magnificent appearance of battle formation, represent the art of the ancient orient which can compare with the art of Rome and Greece.

They are pearls of ancient oriental art and show beauty in three aspects:

Beauty of Scale

The entombed warriors and horses formed a large underground army. Vault I presents a battle formation of infantrymen, chariots and charioteers. Vault II presents a combined battle formation of infantrymen, cavalrymen, chariots and charioteers while Vault III is the headquarters of the army in the Qin Dynasty. The statues of the warriors are

15 – 5   A terra – cotta charioteer

big and strong, and the numbers are large. When you watch them, it seems you are in the battle array of the army, you might see the soldiers ready for battle and hear the horses neighing. They are unprecedented in the history of sculpture of China and the world.

Beauty of Technique

The techniques of making the terra – cotta figures and horses are a combination of sculpture and modeling. The body of the warrior was sculptured with much imagination and the head was modeled and then carved by hand. Several skills such as sculpture, modeling, carving and relief were used. The unearthed terra – cotta figures and horses that you see are greenish grey, but it is not the original colour. The surviving colours on the figures and horses when they were first unearthed included red, white, green, purple and orange – yellow on the robes, black on the armour, pink on the faces, hands and feet. The bright colours made the entombed army look vivid and lively. Unfortunately the original colour can no longer be seen. After being burnt at the time of burial, surrounded by soil for over 2,000 years and weathered after being unearthed, the terra – cotta figures and horses have lost their original colour.

Beauty of Statue

The terra – cotta figures are both realistic and representative in style. Individually, all the terra – cotta figures are alike, motionless and standing upright, but their makers individualised them through different facial expressions and face modeling. The faces of warriors are square jawed with narrow foreheads suggesting power and strength, while most faces of the vanguard have a square forehead and a narrow jaw indicating intelligence. Different configurations of facial features are combined with different face types to create varied facial expressions. Meanwhile the makers differentiated the ranks and types of the soldiers by giving them different uniforms, weapons and postures.

In conclusion, the unique artistic features of the terra – cotta warriors and horses are realism; a sense of movement while motionless; sameness of figure individualised by different

15 - 6　An archer in kneeling position forshooting

facial expressions; a combination of sculpture and carving. The entombed warriors demonstrate the success of large - scale sculpture of ancient China.

XVI. WEAPONS UNEARTHED FROM THE VAULTS OF THE TERRA – COTTA ARMY

The weapons that have been unearthed from the vaults were mainly made of bronze and a few were of iron. There are bronze swords, hooks, halberds, lances, spears, crossbows and arrow heads totaling altogether 40,000 pieces. They can be divided into crossbows, long – handled weapons, short – handled weapons and weapons for guards of honour. In the battle formation most warriors held crossbows and some spears. The combination of long – distant weapons and short – distant weapons can assist and protect groups of soldiers.

LONG – HANDLED WEAPONS

The long – handled weapons held by the terra – cotta warriors are dagger – axes, spears and halberds.

The dagger – axes and spears were the main weapons of the army in the Western Zhou (11th century to 771 B.C.). A historical book records that at the Battle of Muye (a place) – the earliest battle recorded in Chinese history (over 3,000 years ago) – the King of Zhou ordered his soldiers "Hold onto your dagger－axes and spears to attack the enemy".

Dagger－axes have been discovered at many historical sites, but only one bronze dagger－axe has been unearthed from Vault I so far. Compared to other weapons, it indicates that the dagger－axe was not the main weapon used by the State of Qin unlike the Zhou Dynasty.

The spear was one of the ancient weapons for attack. Ten spears have been unearthed from the vaults so far and nine were made of bronze and one of iron. Compared with dagger－axes by quantity, it seemed that the spear was the main weapon of the army instead of the dagger－axe in the Qin Dynasty. They were made of both bronze and iron. The surface of the spear is smooth and the blade is sharp even today.

The halberd was another ancient weapon which combines the advantages of the spear and the dagger－axe. It was one of the best long－handled weapons for both attack and defense. Its handle was 2. 9 metres long. Four halberds have been unearthed from the vaults and on one blade was inscribed Chinese words stating that the halberd was made by workmen in Prime Minister Lu Buwei's Workshop in Year Three of the Qin Dynasty. In later dynasties the halberd was used not only in battle, but also used as a symbol of noble families. In the Tang Dynasty (618 to 907) the halberd was stood in front of the houses of only the top three officials.

The "pi" was a weapon mainly used in the Spring and Autumn Period (770 to 476 B. C.) and the times of the

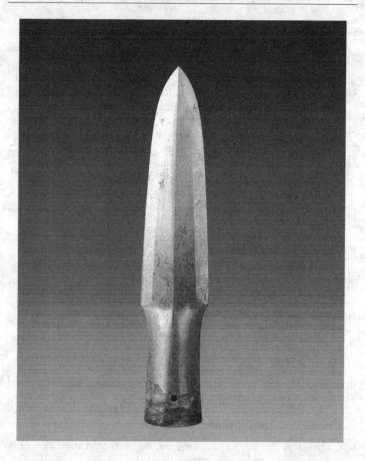

16 – 1   A bronze pike with inscription

Warring States (475 to 221 B.C.). However, it was mistaken for a short sword because historians in the Han Dynasty (206 B.C. to 24 A.D.) described wrongly. The first bronze pi was unearthed in Vault I in 1975, but it was thought to be a short

16 - 2   A bronze Pi

sword. The head of the pi is like a short sword, but it has a
long handle which was 3. 3 to 3. 6 metres long in the Qin
Dynasty. Sixteen pi have been unearthed from the vaults and
most were lying beside a terra - cotta warrior.

16－3   Bronze Shu

Both the "yue" and the "shu" were weapons used by guards of honour. The yue came from the battle axe, but was used as a symbol of special status from the Shang Dynasty (16th to 11th B. C.). It lost its battle function in the Qin Dynasty. The shu was a ceremonial weapon without a blade. About 30 pieces of the shu were excavated from Vault III and a bundle of 20 pieces with one metre of their handles remaining was unearthed in the northern house of Vault III. The shu was cast and then polished. From observation, all the warriors in Vault III held shus. The excavation of Vault III showed that the shu was used as a ceremonial weapon, not a real weapon, in the Qin Dynasty.

SHORT-HANDLED WEAPONS

The use of the sword as an attacking weapon in battle lasted only a short period. The earliest bronze sword discovered in China was made in the Western Zhou Dynasty (11th century to 771 B. C.) and the sword was actively used in the Spring and Autumn Period (770 to 476 B.C.). A sword made in Yue Kingdom in the late Spring and Autumn Period was unearthed from a tomb in Hebei Province. The sword is 55.7 centimetres long and 4.6 centimetres wide, with a handle of 8.4 centimetres. Technical examination reveals that the sword is composed of copper and tin and had been heat treated. Though made over 2,400 years ago, it glittered with metallic lustre without rust when unearthed.

22 bronze swords have been unearthed from the vaults of the Entombed Army, five were broken. The swords are 81 to 94.8 centimetres long with handles of 16 to 21.8 centimetres, and hung at the waists of warriors. The tin contained in swords made in the Qin Dynasty was higher than ones made earlier. The Qin sword is sharp and can cut though 19 pieces of paper put together. It is firm and tenacious and its surface was chromium plated. A sword was found squashed under a terra-cotta figure when it was unearthed in Vault I. It was curved beneath the figure for more than 2,200 years, but sprang

16 - 4   Golden hooks' made of bronze

straight when the figure was removed.

The officer on the No. 1 Bronze Chariot and horses excavated from the Qin Mausoleum Garden had a sword hung at his waist. The sword is 60 centimetres long, half the length

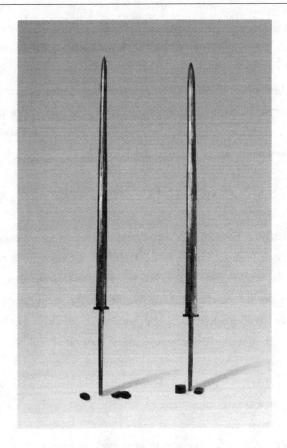

16 - 5 Bronze sword

of the original like the whole chariot and horses. It was
exquisitely made. It is believed that the First Emperor's sword
must have been the best made in the Qin Dynasty.

The hook, also called "the gold hook", is said in a

historical book to have been used popularly from the Spring and Autumn Period (770 to 476 B. C.) to the Song Dynasty (990 to 1279). But a real hook had not been seen until one was unearthed from Vault I of the Entombed Army. Two hooks have been discovered from the vaults to date. Being like knives, they were cast and then polished. Both have two blades and could be used for cutting and hooking.

LONG-RANGE WEAPONS

Both the bow and the crossbow are for firing arrows, but they are different. The bow is stretched and shot by a man's strength while the crossbow is stretched and shot with mechanical force. The bow was one of the earliest weapons invented by human beings and was used as early as the Old Stone Age. At that time arrow heads were made of stone and bone flakes. The first bronze arrow heads appeared in the Shang Dynasty (16th to 11th Century B. C.). The bronze crossbow was an improvement on the bow and could shoot much further.

With the bow, the string is pulled back and fired by the archer's strength, while the crossbow is loaded and fired with mechanical force.

The crossbow unearthed from the vaults of Entombed Army consisted of three parts: the bow, the handle and the arrow – holding mechanism. The bow was originally 1. 3 to 1. 4

metres long, but had rotted away and only the bronze arrow —
holding mechanism remained. From the remains we can judge
there were at least three kinds of crossbow in the Qin Dynasty.

ARMOUR

Apart from the recent discovery of stone armour in a
separate pit, experts have determined from unearthed warriors
that there were several types of armour in the Qin Dynasty.
Armour was a means of judging large or small, strong or weak,
states. Armour was first made of leather and later from metal.
In the Qin Dynasty soldiers had armour to protect the chest,
back, legs, and arms and even horses wore armour. The
armour not only protected the soldier and reduced the death
rate, but also made them look stronger and encouraged them to
fight bravely.

The armour can be divided into six types from the warriors
unearthed from the vaults. It is for warriors, charioteers,
cavalrymen, lower officers, middle level officers and generals.

The warrior's armour is simple and consists of three parts:
front armour, back armour and upper arm covers. The front
armour has eight rows of shingles and the back armour has
seven rows of shingles. The shingles were linked together with
different sewing methods, allowing the warrior to move his
waist and arms easily. The lower officer's armour is almost the
same as the armour of the warrior. But the shingles of armour

are more numerous than those of the warrior showing the higher status. There are eleven rows of shingles in both the front and back armour.

There are two types of armour for middle level officers: one for officers on the chariots and the other for infantry officers. The officers on the chariots only had front armour and two belts linked the armour. They had neither back armour nor upper arm covers. The armour of infantry officers consisted of front armour, back armour and upper arm covers. Both the front and back armour were made of a piece of leather and there are eleven shingles at the edge of the front armour and thirteen shingles at the edge of the back armour. There are a wide margin around the front, back and upper arm covers. The upper arm covers are wider and longer than those of warriors.

The charioteer of different types of chariots wore different armour. The charioteer unearthed from Vault I has the same armour as the lower officer, but without upper arm covers. The charioteers unearthed from Vault II has armour which protected the neck, front, back, arms and the top surface of the hands. The armour covered the arms and the body armour was 80 centimetres long, the same as generals.

The most simple armour of all is that of the cavalryman. The armour is short without arm covers. It meets the need of quick movement of the cavalryman.

The armour of the general is large and luxurious. It consisted of the front armour, back armour and arm covers.

Both the front and back armour is made of a large piece of leather. There are eleven and nine shingles separately at the sides of the front and back armour. The arm cover is made of a piece of leather without any shingles. There are eight belts knotted as flowers on the upper part of the front and back armour, which were painted red, or green in patterns of a rhombus. The general's armour is beautiful and good protection, and no other armours could compare with it.

WONDERS OF METALLURGICAL HISTORY

Chemical analysis of the weapons unearthed from the vaults of the Entombed Army reveal that the weapons contain copper (Cu), tin (Sn) and lead (Pb) mainly, but also iron (Fe), manganese (Mn), magnesium (Mg), cobalt (Co), zinc (Zn), titanium (Ti), chromium (Cr) and molybdenum (Mo). The different proportions of tin in copper produced different hardnesses in the bronze — the higher the tin content, the harder the bronze. The percentage of tin in swords found in the vaults is 18 to 20 percent.

From the unearthed weapons the secret of metallurgical technology of the Qin Dynasty was discovered. The weapons were cast, ground and polished. To prevent rusting, swords and arrow heads were coated with a thin layer (10 micron) of oxidized chromium, which proves they were oxidized with chromium during manufacture. The technology of chromium coating was invented by a German in 1937, by a American who registered in a patent in 1950, but in China the chromium – coating technique was employed in manufacture of weapons over 2, 200 year ago. It is truly a wonder of metallurgical history. The weapons coated with chromium were still bright and sharp without rust when they were unearthed though they had been buried for over 2,200 years.

On the surface of the bronze pi there are patterns of irregular clouds which were neither cast, nor engraved. The patterns are apart the weapon and appear on the surface, but there are no engraving marks. Experts have inferred that they were produced during forging at high temperature. This technique can be listed as a wonder in the history of Chinese metallurgy.

It has also been discovered that hundreds of crossbow triggers, whose suspending knives and bolts can be used interchangeably, had a tolerance error of 1 millimetre. The arrow heads are divided into four types. The outline of the three sides of the arrow heads of the same type has a tolerance error of 0. 15 millimetre. From this, we can see that weapon manufacture was already standardized to meet the needs of war. It also shows that Chinese metallurgical technology had reached a high standard and ranked first in the world during the Qin Dynasty.

XVII. THE TERRA – COTTA ARMY
IN FOREIGNERS' EYES

With the excavation and exhibition of Vault I, II and III of the Qin First Emperor's Terra – cotta Army, the Museum became a tourist attraction and draws more and more tourists from abroad. It is said, "If you go to China without going to Shaanxi, it means you haven't been to China. If you go to Shaanxi without going to the Museum of the Qin First Emperor's Terra – cotta Warriors and Horses, it means you haven't been to Shaanxi".

THE FIRST PERSON TO INTRODUCE
THE TERRA—COTTA ARMY TO THE WORLD

The Terra – cotta Army was discovered during the turmoil of the "Cultural Revolution". For its announcement to the world and the following sensation one must thank the journalist, Audrey Topping. Audrey's father was an old China hand. Born in 1884 in China he served in the country as a missionary in the 1920s. He later became a Canadian diplomat and friend of the late Chinese Premier Zhou Enlai. Because of this connection, Audrey was invited to visit China several times, and in 1978 went with her father and sister to Xi'an, where she obtained special permission to visit the Terra－cotta Army Museum, which had just begun to be built. She saw newly unearthed terra － cotta figures, interviewed archaeologists on site, and wrote and filed her report back home that night.

In her article Audrey gives a good overview of the Qin First Emperor － － － his historic exploit of uniting China, his policies to increase population, his brutal treatment of scholars, his giant and wasteful tomb project, his terra－cotta army and his cruel treatment of the tomb's builders. Her article was supported by over 10 colour pictures of the terra － cotta army supplied by the Xinhua News Agency and appeared in the April, 1978 issue of "National Geographic" as the cover story. Given the reputation of the magazine, news of this discovery in China spread quickly all over the world. Most of American and European tourists who went to Xi'an in the late 1970s were drawn by Audrey's article.

A nine year old boy student from America wrote a letter to the Director of the Museum in 1992 saying he and his class were amazed and eager to know more of the new excavation of the terra－cotta army when they read Audrey's article.

THE TERRA—COTTA FIGURES FIRST
WITNESSED BY FOREIGNERS

The terra—cotta figures were first witnessed by foreigners two years after they were discovered. In May 1976 the Prime Minister of Singapore, Lee Kuan Yew, who was visiting China at the time, heard of the discovery and asked to visit the excavation site. When he reached Vault I, he was so astonished by what he saw, he did not utter a word. But before he left, he said, "The discovery of the terra—cotta figures and horses is one of the wonders of the world, something the Chinese nation can be proud of".

Lee Kuan Yew visited the Museum of the Terra—cotta Warriors and Horses of Qin Shihuang again on September 17, 1985. He was pleased to see the new discoveries and the ongoing excavation of the Entombed Army.

THE EIGHTH WONDER OF THE WORLD

The eighth wonder of the world has become another description of the terra—cotta vaults since the late 1970s. There is a story of why it is so called.

On September 23, 1978, the Mayor of Paris, Jacques Chirac, visited the site of Vault I where construction of the hall and excavation were going on simultaneously. When he saw the magnificent Terra – cotta Army he remarked, "The world used to have seven wonders. The discovery of the Terra – cotta Army can be said to be the eighth. You can't say you've been to Egypt without seeing the pyramids. Now you can't say you've been to China without seeing the Terra – cotta Army". Two nearby reporters, one from "AFP", the French News Agency, and the other from "Le Monde", quoted his remarks in their stories which were published in Paris. Since then the eighth wonder of the world became known to the world and has spread. On November 5, 1991 then President of France, Jacques Chirac visited the museum a second time. He confirmed his remarks as he wrote his impressions, "This visit confirmed it is the eighth wonder of the world really. Its long historical culture and art can compare with the ancient capitals such as Athens, Rome and Babylon".

THE TERRA–COTTA ARMY VISITED
BY MANY HEADSOF GOVERNMENT
FROM FOREIGN COUNTRIES

The Terra – cotta Warriors and Horses attract visitors from both China and abroad. At the time of writing, the Museum has received more than 40 million visitors since it opened to the public, one – tenth from overseas. Many presidents and heads of government from foreign countries have visited the Entombed Army.

On October 16, 1989 Elizabeth II, Queen of the United Kingdom came to visit the Entombed Army. As she alighted from the car, she saw "terra – cotta warriors" standing in lines in front of the Exhibition Hall. She was excited to approach the "terra – cotta warriors", but found they moved. She was astonished until told the "terra – cotta warriors" were actors. When she went down into Vault I, she watched the real terra – cotta warriors carefully. She said, "I heard of the entombed warriors and horses, and saw photos of them in the past, but I see them now and they are truly wonderful".

17 – 1   Bill Clinton, President of the US visiting the Museum of
          Entombed Army

Bill Clinton, President of the United States visited the Museum of the Entombed Army on June 25, 1998. When he arrived at the Museum, he told Director Wu Yongqi, "Since I first heard of the Entombed Warriors and Horses being excavated near Xi'an 20 years ago I have had a desire to visit them. Now I'm here". Clinton was given special permission to go down into Vault I "to inspect the underground army of 2200 years ago" said the Director. In the Restoration Centre, the Director asked the President to fix the head of a warrior, which had just been restored, to its body. Clinton was pleased and fitted it carefully. He said he was glad to take part in the restoration of the Terra – cotta Warriors. It was planned for Clinton to stay at the Museum for one and a half hours, but he stayed for three.

XVIII. THREE STORIES ASSOCIATED WITH THE TERRA – COTTA ARMY AND ITS MUSEUM

There are interesting stories about the discovery and excavation of the terra – cotta figures and their Museum.

WHAT KIND OF INSTRUMENT WAS USED TO EXPLORE THE TERRA – COTTA FIGURES?

When you visit the terra – cotta warriors and horses, you

18 – 1   Louyang spade, a special tool for archaeological excavation

may wonder what kind of advanced instrument was used to explore and excavate them. It is a simple tool — a "Louyang spade". Archaeological workers used the spade to determine the extent of Vault I and to discover Vault II and III and over 100 pits of burial objects around the Qin Tumulus.

There is a story about the spade. In the Han Dynasty, Liu Zhang was entitled King of Yangcheng (now Louyang City — 350 km east of Xi'an) by Emperor Wendi in 180 B. C. He chose Mount Beimong, north of Louyang, as his burial place and built his tomb there because the mountain was considered a place of good "fengshui" (geomantic omen). Later, many nobles of different dynasties built their tombs there, resulting in the mountain being covered in tombs. When digging a new tomb, people often dug out old tombs. Fengshui Masters had to ask people to dig down a metre in the earth to make sure nothing was there before deciding on a site for a new tomb. During the reign of Jiaqing of the Qing Dynasty, a blacksmith named Ma invented a U — shaped spade, two cun (1 cun = 3.3 centimetres) wide and about a foot long, with a long, narrow opening in the centre. The top was connected to a two — metre bamboo pole. The spade could be pushed three or four cun into the earth. When pulled out, it would bring up earth of different layers, as they originally occurred. A study of the earth sample, its structure, colour, density, contents and smell, revealed the below surface situation. If the earth had been disturbed, something must have been buried there. If the spade came across something foreign, the sample would show what it was. Experienced people could tell what was under the surface simply by pushing the spade into the earth.

Large scale construction occurred around Luoyang City in the 1950s. There were many cultural relics and historical remains underground because Luoyang had been the capital of 6 dynasties in ancient China. To find whether there were cultural relics or historical remains on a site, the spade was used for exploring before construction. In 1954, Luoyang City organized an excavation training session to promote the spade (which it called "the Luoyang spade") in archaeological circles. As with the excavation of the Qin Entombed Army, many excavations across China relied on this spade.

WHO INSCRIBED THE NAME OF THE MUSEUM?

When you visit Chinese places of interest, you may come across inscriptions by well – known people from former dynasties or from modern times. These examples of Chinese calligraphic art are as valuable as the places of interest. So it is with the Museum of the First Emperor's Terra – cotta Warriors and Horses.

The name of the Museum was inscribed by Marshal Ye Jianying. Marshal Ye strongly supported a proposal to build a protective and exhibition hall on Vault I soon after the terra – cotta figures were discovered. On April 9, 1979 Ye Jianying,

秦始皇兵馬俑博物館

葉劍英

一九七九年

九月十日

18-2　Name of the Museum written by Marshal Ye Jianying

then Vice Chairman of the Central Committee of the Chines Communist Party, came to the excavation site which was the first inspection by this high Chinese leader. Marshal Ye, one of the ten marshals in China who had taken part in numerous battles, showed a great interest in the underground army. He carefully scrutinised the warriors and horses and the weapons, such as spears, crossbows, swords and arrow – heads in the temporary exhibition room. Afterwards Mr. Yang, a leader in the Preparation Division of the Museum asked Marshal Ye to do the inscription of the name of the Museum saying, "This is the museum of the terra – cotta army and you are a marshal. It's appropriate for you to inscribe the name." Ye agreed, but said he would not do it until the third anniversary of Chairman Mao's death (Chairman Mao Zedong died on September 9, 1976). In September 1979, just after the third anniversary, Marshal Ye inscribed the name "The Museum of the Qin First Emperor's Terra – cotta Warriors and Horses" and mailed it to the Museum.

The Museum, with its name inscribed by Marshal Ye, was officially opened to the public on October 1, 1979, the Thirtieth Anniversary of the founding of the People's Republic of China.

A THIEF STOLE A HEAD OF A TERRA – COTTA FIGURE, BUT LOST HIS OWN HEAD

As the terra – cotta figures became more and more famous after the 1970s, they also became a target for theft because of their value.

On the night of February 27, 1987, it was cold and quiet. A thief named Wang Gengdi quietly climbed the wall and entered the courtyard of the archaeological squad without being noticed by the guards. He pried open a storage building and stole a head of a terra – cotta general. He slipped away like a ghost and hid the head in a forest north of Lintong Railway Station at a spot chosen during day time. The stolen head was one of the ten unearthed master pieces of the terra – cotta generals, which had been listed in Category A, the highest class of the National Cultural Relics.

Wang was a 21 year old local peasant who didn't like farming. He had gone to the railway station to do some temporary labouring work, where he saw people who became wealthy by selling tourist souvenirs. He wanted to follow their example and was noticed by another railway worker named Quan Xueli. One day in January, the two got together and while drinking talked about selling terra – cotta figures to make money.

After Wang had stolen the head of a terra – cotta general, he told Quan who had little knowledge of cultural relics. Quan was surprised and pleased to find it a very valuable treasure. They looked for a dealer to sell the head, but when negotiating a price of 300,000 Yuan RMB (US $ 37,500), at an inn in Xi'an on June 17, they were all arrested.

Wang was sentenced to death by the Court. He was the

first criminal executed for stealing cultural relics in Shaanxi Province after 1949. Quan was also punished.

XIX. RESTORATION AND PROTECTION OF THE TERRA - COTTA STATUES

The Qin Mausoleum and its attendant vaults, including the vaults of terra - cotta warrior and horses, are a treasure of China and have been listed as part of the World's Cultural Legacy. They are under the National Protection. Excavation and restoration of the terra - cotta warriors and horses hasn't halted since they were unearthed, but the restoration is not an easy task.

RESTORATION OF THE TERRA-COTTA STATUES

The Entombed Warriors were severely damaged by fire and by pressure of the earth for 2,200 years. There was not one complete warrior or horse when excavated. They were all broken into pieces.

How are they being restored? When a terra-cotta figure is found, archaeological workers make a record of the location, its situation and the relationship between it and surrounding figures. They also take photos and mark numbers on the figures. Before restoration, the workers make a study of the figure to understand its structure and attachments. Then a plan

19 – 1   Terra – cotta warriors being excavated

for the process and method of restoration is made. The restoration involves careful scientific work. The following is a simple description of the restoration process.

Firstly, the archaeological workers classify the unearthed fragments of a warrior according to shape, patterns and colours, and then they attempt to match the fragments and put marks on them.

Secondly, with a small knife or brush, the workers remove earth from the fragments, especially from the fragment's edges, and then clean them with water. The fragments are left to dry.

Thirdly, the workers clean the edges with a fluid, and paint them with epoxy resin to glue the pieces together from the bottom upwards. While being glued, the figure is separated into several parts to allow it to solidify without the glue breaking. Reinforcing struts are put inside the legs to support them. Glued pieces of cloth are stuck over the inside of joints to strengthen them.

Fourthly, after the glued fragments are dry, the joint lines are covered over.

Fifthly, the figure is made to look as old as it is.

Finally the restored figure is placed at its original spot when unearthed.

All the terra – cotta warriors and horses are carefully restored by dozens of methods.

SIX KNEELING COLOURED TERRA – COTTA ARCHERS AND A GREEN – FACED TERRA – COTTA WARRIOR WERE RECENTLY UNEARTHED

As the first stage of the excavation of Vault II earth was removed from the ruined rafters. During 1999 they commenced the second stage to excavate the terra – cotta warriors and horses under the ruined rafters. Six kneeling painted terra – cotta archers in poses of firing and a green – faced archer were found. The colours on the archers are well preserved. At the time of writing some of these archers have been unearthed and some partly unearthed. It is unprecedented to discover the warriors with well preserved colours. For various reasons, the colour dropped off the terra - cotta warriors and horses when unearthed. The new discovery is exciting news. In order to allow visitors to clearly watch the newly discovered kneeling archers, four telescopes have been installed on the edge of Vault II.

The composition of colours on painted parts are different. Some archers had a gelatin coating first and then pigments were applied in one or two layers. Some archers had a gelatin coating on some parts without colour painting. The archers were painted with various colours. Faces are pink and the necks are pinkish green. Hands are pinkish white or red and the robes are green. The legs are pinkish green or red and the hair is black. The eyes were first painted white and black was used to mark out the pupils. The brightly coloured archers are masterpieces for they convey a feeling of action and vigor.

On September 10, 1999, a warrior was found with a green face except for its black hair, beard and eyes. It is the first such discovery since excavation of the Entombed Army began. Unlike other warriors with pinkish - red or pinkish - white faces, this is a green - faced warrior. Some said this is the result of a chemical reaction of the colour with other materials buried underground for such a long time. Others argued it was painted by a craftsman imitating the dark - skinned people. Yet others said it is made by a craftsman as a practical joke. Which saying is correct? Further study is required.

19-2   The colored head of a warrior

SCIENTIFIC PROTECTION OF
THE TERRA—COTTA STATUES

Protection of the colours on the terra — cotta warriors and horses is a core task in the conservation of the terra — cotta

19 - 3   The colored head of a warrior

figures. After many years of hard work, archaeologists have achieved a break - through. The composition of the colours throughout has been analyzed and the main composition of the first layer is Chinese raw lacquer. The main reason for the colour damage is that the Chinese raw lacquer begins to roll up when the terra - cotta clay is dry. This causes the colours to drop off the terra - cotta figures. Now the archaeologists have

19 - 4   The colored head of a warrior

found an effective means of protection. When a protective liquid is sprayed onto the painted terra – cotta figures several times, the colours do not fall off. This method is now used in the excavations of Vault II.

The excavation and the successful protection of the kneeling painted archers are of great importance. They will reveal the original colours of the terra – cotta warriors and horses and provide experts with valuable data for the study of paint technology, colour of clothing and composition of colours in the Qin Dynasty.

When studying the composition of the colours, experts found a chemical mixture called "copper barium silicate" in the colour purple. It was quite a surprise as this compound was a by – product of studying synthesized super – conductive materials in the 1980s. It has not been found in nature. This determination shows that Chinese people had mastered a technique to make a mixed material by a synthesizing method 2,200 years ago. Is this another wonder in the history of science and technology. How this material was produced requires further research.

POSTSCRIPT

By Zhang Tao

People both at home and abroad have become more and more interested in the Entombed Army since it was discovered in 1970s, specially when the kneeling painted terra - cotta archers were excavated and successfully protected in Vault II, and vaults of stone armour, semi - naked terra - cotta figures depicting theatrical performers and a large tripod of the Qin Dynasty were excavated in the Qin mausoleum garden in late 1990s.

Thanks to Mr. Liu Daoxun in the Foreign Affairs Office of the Xianyang Municipal People's Government, Shaanxi Province, who has translated the book into English, and Mr. Robert Dorning from Australia, who has proof - read the book, the book has been well done. They not only translated and proof read the book, but also gave some constructive suggestions to make the book successful.

The book introduces systematically the history of the Qin Dynasty, China's First Emperor, the Qin Mausoleum, the Terra-cotta Warriors and Horses, new discoveries, and you may like to read. You are welcome to give your suggestions and comments to improve the book in the next edit. You can write to: Zhang Tao, The Museum of Terra-cotta Warriors and Horses of Qin Shihuang, Lintong County, Shaanxi Province, P. R. China, 710600, you may also send an E-mail to me: taozhang@pub. xaonline. com; zt1965@263. net